D1526534

Human Trafficking
in the Midwest

Human Trafficking in the Midwest

A Case Study of St. Louis and the Bi-State Area

Erin C. Heil

Southern Illinois University Edwardsville

Andrea J. Nichols

Washington University in St. Louis

Carolina Academic Press

Durham, North Carolina

Copyright © 2015
Carolina Academic Press
All Rights Reserved

Library of Congress Cataloging-in-Publication Data

Heil, Erin C.
Human trafficking in the Midwest : a case study of St. Louis
and the bi-state area / Erin C. Heil and Andrea J. Nichols.
  pages cm
Includes bibliographical references and index.
ISBN 978-1-61163-638-3 (alk. paper)
1. Human trafficking--Missouri--St. Louis--Case studies. 2.
Human trafficking--Missouri--Case studies. 3. Human traffick-
ing--Illinois--Case studies. I. Nichols, Andrea J. II. Title.

HQ146.S2H45 2015
306.3'620977865--dc23

2014049541

Portions of chapters 3 and 4 were first published in:
Nichols, Andrea J. and Heil, Erin. 2014. Challenges to Identify-
ing and Prosecuting Sex Trafficking Cases in the Midwest United
States. 9n2, 1–30, *Feminist Criminology*.

Carolina Academic Press
700 Kent Street
Durham, NC 27701
Telephone (919) 489-7486
Fax (919) 493-5668
www.cap-press.com

Printed in the United States of America
2015 Reprint

Contents

Acknowledgments

First and foremost, we would like to thank all of the individuals that assisted in this project, including the local- and federal-level legal officials, social service providers, and survivors. This book would have not been possible without your stories and experiences with human trafficking.

We would like to thank our editor, Beth Hall. She fully supported this project from the initial proposal, and guided us throughout the process.

We would like to thank our friends and family who remained patient with our absence through travel and constant writings. They listened to us as we tackled new ideas, and fully supported this endeavor when it was nothing more than a discussion between the two of us.

Human Trafficking in the Midwest

Chapter 1

Introduction

"I was taken from my doorstep ... I was sold for sex with men in exchange for money and drugs. I was forced to work out of motels, brothels, prostitution houses, and massage parlors. I tried to run so many times but I never seemed to be able to escape without getting caught and beat up. I have had chains wrapped around my ankles, wrists, and neck, like a dog. I got beat up with baseball bats, crow bars, basically anything that they [could] get their hands on." These words were spoken by a brave survivor in front of hundreds of listeners attending an anti-human trafficking event. Although her voice shook and she read from her handwritten script, she stood strong in the face of her victimization. She wanted her story to be heard, and more importantly, she wanted to be seen. She looked up from her small piece of paper, looked the audience in the eyes, and proudly stated, "I refuse to believe what the world labels me as. I refuse to believe that I am trash. I refuse to believe I'm good for one thing only. I refuse to believe that nobody loves me. I refuse to believe that I'm not beautiful. I refuse to believe that I am nothing." Although these were the words of emotional torture she was told while she was being sold for sex, she had survived, and she was able to victoriously tell her story.

A local FBI agent stoically speaks of the long hours of surveillance that led to the successful prosecution of ten individuals who held and controlled 16 young women in a sex trafficking ring. He does not hesitate to speak of the beatings the girls endured, the constant dominance the girls faced from their various "traffickers" and buyers. He proudly boasts that the leader of this trafficking ring was sentenced to 50 years in prison. He has told this story many times, and has removed himself from the emotional aspect of investigating human trafficking cases. That is, until he speaks

3

of the youngest of the victims in this trafficking ring. She was a mentally disabled 12-year-old girl who was sold numerous times a day, every day. Through surveillance, it was observed that every time this little girl was sold for sex, she took along with her a teddy bear to provide her with her own sense of safety and security. At this point, the FBI officer stopped speaking, wiped the tears from his face, and the reality came to those who listened that these victims were more than numbers or stories for media hype, but children who were very afraid and very alone. More importantly, he became more than a federal law enforcement agent, but a man who humanized each of his identified survivors. He cried for them, sympathized with their pain, and was personally affected by the cases he investigated.

Migrant workers travel across the country only to find that in order to secure work, they must pay in advance for a labor position at a farm or orchard. This, in turn, leads to an already existing debt before the work even begins. The workers, unable to afford a suitable living space, are found in overcrowded trailers, porches, or hotel rooms. Completely lost in the middle of nowhere, with no way to overcome the language barriers with local officials, the migrant laborers find themselves in a situation of debt bondage equivalent to modern day slavery. Extremely fearful of physical retribution by the farmhands or the threat of deportation, very few of these migrant laborers seek help, and therefore find it impossible to escape their situation. Advocates speak of the few that seek assistance, whether it is for food, medicine, or legal advice, and the reality of their labor trafficking is conveyed to those who listen. Because of the hidden nature of labor trafficking, the stories that are revealed are few, for the migrants move with the seasonal harvest, and many are too proud to seek out any available help regardless of inescapable debt, physical and psychological abuses, and deplorable living and working conditions.

The above scenarios are not from films or distant countries, but were told to us by survivors, advocates, and legal personnel that we met, interviewed, presented with, or simply observed in events and trainings as we systematically researched and unraveled the reality of human trafficking in St. Louis, Missouri, and the surrounding bi-state area. This book is a compilation of the voices involved in the anti-human trafficking movement in the St. Louis bi-state area; from survivors, to advocates, to local and federal legal agents. The purpose of this book is not to re-exploit the victims by sensationalizing their stories, but rather to provide a complete picture of the sex and labor trafficking evident in this region of the Midwest. These examples each provide a small piece of the larger puzzle, and the readers will soon see the complexity of the wide spectrum of human trafficking in its multifaceted forms. Additionally, we intend to highlight the immense work of advocates and legal professionals, in identifying and protecting survivors while punishing the offenders. Further, the book examines areas of human trafficking that have received little attention in the academic and public discourse; including labor trafficking, pornography-as-trafficking, and the trafficking or commercial sexual exploitation of LGBTQ people, men and boys. Much of the Midwest is overlooked when discussing domestic human trafficking, and by specifically examining the St. Louis bi-state area, this book will not only expose that human trafficking is occurring in the heartland of the United States, but more importantly, that parts of the Midwest have become source, destination, and transit sites of human trafficking.

Definitions

As we began researching human trafficking in the most general sense, we found that there was variation in anti-trafficking legislation and related definitions between states, as well as between state and federal governments. This discrepancy, in turn, determined what was and what was not being identified as human trafficking. The majority of those interviewed for this project referred to the legal code when discussing human trafficking, but even this can become problematic as state laws vary from each other, as well as from the federal definitions.

According to the federal Trafficking Victims Protection Act
(TVPA) of 2000, and its reauthorizations in 2003, 2005, 2008, and
2013, a severe form of trafficking is defined as,

> a. a commercial sex act induced by force, fraud, or coer-
> cion, or in which the person induced to perform such act
> has not attained 18 years of age; or
> b. the recruitment, harboring, transportation, provision,
> or obtaining of a person for labor or services, through the
> use of force, fraud, or coercion for the purpose of subjec-
> tion to involuntary servitude, peonage, debt bondage, or
> slavery. (TVPA, Section 103, 8a and b)

Section a. is typically used to define sex trafficking, while section b. is often used to define labor trafficking. In addition, also
on a federal level, 18 U.S.C. § 1581 of Title 18 outlines the various
labor trafficking offenses, including: peonage, involuntary servitude, and forced labor. The unlawful act of peonage is defined as
"hold[ing] a person in 'debt servitude,' or peonage, which is closely
related to involuntary servitude" (18 U.S.C. § 1581. Section 1581
of Title 18). Involuntary servitude is defined as holding a person
in a "condition of compulsory service or labor against his/her will"
(18 U.S.C. § 1584. Section 1584 of Title 18). The code makes it unlawful to "provide or obtain the labor or services of a person
through [force, fraud or coercion]" (18 U.S.C. § 1589. Section 1589
of Title 18). Taken together, the code criminalizes acts of harboring, recruiting, transporting, or brokering persons for the purpose
of exploitation by means of force, threat of force, coercion, or
threat of legal coercion (18 U.S.C. § 1581. Title 18).

Additionally, the federal criminal code specifically defines sex
trafficking of children by force, fraud, or coercion (18 U.S.C.
§ 1591. Section 1591), which distinguishes the act of sex trafficking
by age. The code defines sex trafficking as "as causing a person to
engage in a commercial sex act under certain statutorily enumerated
conditions," and defines commercial sex act as "any sex act, on account of which anything of value is given to or received by any person" (ibid.). Additionally, the code specifies the requirements for

children involved in a commercial sex act by which something of value is given or received by age, which states that the elements of force, fraud, and coercion are not necessary for a human trafficking charge if the child is under the age of 18. Sex trafficking of adults is based upon whether a commercial sex act was induced by force, fraud, or coercion, as indicated in the TVPA section 8a.

Generally, the state laws in Illinois and Missouri mirror the federal regulations of human trafficking. However, there are some distinct differences that determine whether law enforcement and prosecutors will decide if an identified trafficking case should be tried at the state or federal level. Given that the target of this study was Missouri and Illinois, we will only focus on these state laws. According to Illinois State Law 720 ILCS5/10-9:

> A person commits trafficking in persons when he or she knowingly: (1) recruits, entices, harbors, transports, provides, or obtains by any means, or attempts to recruit, entice, harbor, transport, provide, or obtain by any means, another person, intending or knowing that the person will be subjected to involuntary servitude; or (2) benefits, financially or by receiving anything of value, from participation in a venture that has engaged in an act of involuntary servitude or involuntary sexual servitude of a minor (Accessed September, 2014).

One key component of the Illinois law is the exclusion of the phrase "for the purpose of" and highlights a requisite "knowingly" intent. The term "knowingly" legally holds that the offender is aware of a potential outcome, even if that may not be the desired result. In other words, for human trafficking to occur, state prosecutors must show that the trafficker is aware of the possibility that he/she may be involved in a trafficking situation, rather than purposefully or specifically intending to traffic an individual or individuals. Although there is a slight difference, legally it allows for more prosecutorial room to charge on the basis of "willful blindness," rather than building a case on purposeful or specific intent, which generally is a more evidentiary burden for the prosecutor. However, crimes with the requisite purposeful intent (i.e., "for the purpose of exploitation") generally carry a harsher punishment than those with an associated "knowing" intent. Therefore, given the amount of evidence, prosecutors must make the determination as to whether the case can successfully be charged at the federal level, or if there is only enough evidence to be charged at the state level.

The Missouri statute, very much like the Illinois statute, broadens the scope of the legal definition of human trafficking. The statute defines labor trafficking as:

> A person commits the crime of trafficking for the purposes of slavery, involuntary servitude, peonage, or forced labor if a person knowingly recruits, entices, harbors, transports, provides, or obtains by any means, including but not limited to through the use of force, abduction, coercion, fraud, deception, blackmail, or causing or threatening to cause financial harm, another person for labor or services, for the purposes of slavery, involuntary servitude, peonage, or forced labor, or benefits, financially or by receiving anything of value, from participation in such activities (RSMO, Chapter 566.206, 2013).

The Missouri statute allows for more interpretation with regards to the required intent in that it states both "knowingly" and "for the purpose of." Beyond this dichotomy, what is unique about the Missouri statute is the extension of the "means" requirement. Not only does the statute include force, fraud, or coercion as "means," but also blackmail, abduction, deception, or causing or threatening to cause financial harm. Additionally, the statute clearly states that the "means" requirement is not limited to the given examples, thereby allowing leeway for prosecutors if they determine an act fits under the umbrella requirement of means.

With regards to sex trafficking, the Missouri statute differentiates between trafficking for purposes of sexual exploitation and the sexual trafficking of the child, addressing both adult and child sex trafficking. The former states that:

> A person commits the crime of trafficking for the purposes of sexual exploitation if a person knowingly

recruits, entices, harbors, transports, provides, or obtains by any means, including but not limited to through the use of force, abduction, coercion, fraud, deception, blackmail, or causing or threatening to cause financial harm, another person for the use or employment of such person in sexual conduct, a sexual performance, or the production of explicit sexual material as defined in section 573.010, without his or her consent, or benefits, financially or by receiving anything of value, from participation in such activities (RSMO Chapter 566.209, 2013).

Whereas RSMO Chapter 566.212 (2013) states:

A person commits the crime of sexual trafficking of a child if the individual knowingly: (1) Recruits, entices, harbors, transports, provides, or obtains by any means, including but not limited to through the use of force, abduction, coercion, fraud, deception, blackmail, or causing or threatening to cause financial harm, a person under the age of eighteen to participate in a commercial sex act, a sexual performance, or the production of explicit sexual material..., or benefits, financially or by receiving anything of value, from participation in such activities; or (2) Causes a person under the age of eighteen to engage in a commercial sex act, a sexual performance, or the production of explicit sexual material.

Unlike the other Missouri statutes regarding human trafficking, the crime of sexual trafficking of a child clearly indicates the requisite "knowing" intent. This is imperative, because RSMO 566.212 clearly states that "It shall not be a defense that the defendant believed that the person was eighteen years of age or older" (ibid.).

Although there are unique differences between the various definitions, each piece of legislation retains the general components of act, means, and purpose. A person must be harbored, recruited, transported, or brokered by the means of force, fraud or coercion for the purposes of labor or sexual exploitation. This is true for all definitions with the exception of child sex trafficking, which states that the "means" element is not necessary to prove, if the child is under the age of 18. Given that, we relied on the expertise of those interviewed for this project in that we define human trafficking based on their experience with victims and survivors, as well as the offenders. In other words, dependent on how the case was perceived, whether or not it met state or federal criteria, we define human trafficking in its most general sense allowing for case-by-case interpretations by social service providers and actors in the legal arena, which the reader will see represented in the narratives and related analysis throughout this book.

Prevalence

Given the complexities of defining human trafficking, one can imagine how this affects various dynamics related to accurately documenting prevalence in St. Louis and the bi-state area. Such issues related to systematically researching and estimating prevalence are reflected throughout the entire United States (Clawson et al., 2008; Farrell et al., 2012; Clawson et al., 2006). Estimating prevalence is problematized primarily due to definitional issues, as well as the way such issues are interpreted and implemented by various actors in the justice system. These key issues profoundly impact successful prosecutions, misidentification as another type of crime, and the mobility and hidden nature of human trafficking. The presentation of human trafficking prevalence estimates may also be skewed to reflect biases and interests, specifically with policy makers and advocates.

As already discussed, state and federal legislation differ in the way human trafficking is defined, which will in turn impact prosecutions. On the informal side of definitions is how certain activities are defined as human trafficking. For example, some advocates argue that all forms of prostitution are sex trafficking, while others argue that there are some sex workers that are self-employed and are not being forced or coerced for the purposes of sexual exploitation (Doezema, 1999, 2005; Madden-Dempsey, 2011; Ekberg, 2004; Weitzer, 2010; Oselin, 2014; Nichols, 2015). Thus, those anti-trafficking advocates who fall within the abolitionist camp of "all prostitution is sex trafficking" are going to report much larger numbers of sexually exploited women, men, and children than those who differentiate between prostitution and sex trafficking. On the other hand, some neoliberals who argue that prostitution is distinct from sex trafficking may all but deny the existence of sex trafficking (Doezema, 1999, 2005; Schaeffer-Grabiel, 2010; Weitzer, 2010). In this book, we take an inductive approach, letting the words of our research participants guide the tone of the book rather than adhering to a particular ideological camp to illustrate the complexity and realities of human trafficking in the St. Louis bi-state area.

Misidentification is closely related to definitional issues. As already stated, some advocates may argue that certain cases of prostitution are being misidentified as sex trafficking and vice versa. However, actors in the legal arena may be misidentifying sex trafficking as prostitution, and may also fail to identify its co-occurrence with other related offenses, such as rape, domestic violence, and various drug offenses often associated with sex trafficking victimization, thereby criminalizing the victim (Nichols & Heil, 2014). Although trainings in the identification of victims of human trafficking are provided to law enforcement, the trend to shift local level officers' perceptions of prostitutes from criminals to victims has been slow (Farrell et al., 2012; Clawson, Dutch, & Cummings, 2006). The same is true when law enforcement officers approach possible victims of labor trafficking, especially those individuals that are undocumented (Hopper, 2004; Heil, 2012). Again, there is available training to question and identify foreign nationals who may be victims of labor trafficking, but it is still difficult for many first responders to look past issues of immigration (Nichols & Heil, 2014; Heil, 2012; Hepburn & Simon, 2012). In such cases, trafficking victims may be criminalized as illegal immigrants. The issues with misidentification affect the prevalence rates, in that many potential victims are pushed through the criminal justice system as criminals.

In addition to issues of misidentification and conflicting definitions comes the problem of prosecutorial charges. As will be discussed in later chapters, prosecutors have the overall agenda to win a case. Given that, they are forced to use what evidence they have before them. Because of the "means" element of human trafficking, this charge has shown to be incredibly difficult to prove (Clawson et al., 2008; Farrell et al., 2013). As a result, prosecutors many times will prosecute a potential human trafficking case as another offense, such as sexual assault, pimping, enticement of a minor into prostitution, kidnapping, or a wage per hour violation in order to convict the offender. Although these charges are more likely to result in a successful conviction for the prosecutors, the possibility that these cases are human trafficking cases becomes legally irrelevant. Policy makers and other interested parties may search for successful prosecutions of human trafficking in St. Louis and the bi-state area and find that only a handful of cases have actually been prosecuted, thereby skewing the reality of the prevalence of human trafficking (Farrell et al., 2012; Nichols & Heil, 2014).

Lastly, the constant movement of the traffickers and victims affects prevalence estimates. Although movement is not required for the label of trafficking, a barrier to identifying human trafficking is mobility. In order to protect themselves from identification and punishment, traffickers will not stay in one location for long. They must move the victims from one location to another to maintain a profit, yet remain under the radar of advocates and law enforcement. Thus, trafficking will go through a general ebb and flow, moving with the demand. For example, sex trafficking may increase when the city hosts a large sporting event, but then may quiet down as traffickers move victims to another location that shows high demand. With regards to labor trafficking, victims will be moved with the jobs. Labor trafficking, especially in the agricultural sector, is dependent on the season and the harvest. Some agricultural communities will not show evidence of labor trafficking only because the season has passed and the victims have been transferred to another location, or workers are migrating with the possibility of employment. Therefore, researchers interested in prevalence cannot just pick one point in time to investigate human trafficking, but rather need to focus on the trends and the movement of traffickers and victims.

Given the problems associated with prevalence, to give an accurate number of human trafficking victims in St. Louis and the bi-state area would be a misnomer. However, St. Louis has been identified by the federal government as "one of the top 20 human trafficking jurisdictions" (Raasch, 2014). One main reason that St. Louis has been identified as a hub for human trafficking is because of its "middle-America location on interstate highways and its constant hosting of big sporting and entertainment events...," both of which provide for a "destination and layover in the sex trafficking trade" (ibid). On the east side of the Mississippi River are various adult entertainment venues that thrive on sexual imagery and fantasy, allowing for traffickers to tap into an already existing pool of potential clients. Additionally, in St. Louis and the bi-state area, there is a large number of runaway youth, as well as isolated immigrant communities, both of which traffickers prey on in order to maintain a profitable group of victims. In neighboring agricultural communities, migrant labor flourishes in orchards and processing plants. Throughout this research, we agreed that we are uncomfortable in presenting an actual number estimating how often human trafficking is occurring. However, given its location in middle America, as well as the social and economic situations that foster human trafficking, we are confident in stating that the identified instances of human trafficking in St. Louis and the bi-state area are not fringe cases, but rather one layer of a thriving underworld that is hidden and often misidentified, as the narratives in this book illustrate throughout.

Identified Research Gaps

Human trafficking is currently a hot topic of discussion both socially and in academia. Researchers, students, and journalists are quickly coming to realize that human trafficking is a very real phenomenon occurring within the borders of the United States. Victims are both domestic citizens and foreign nationals, each with his or her story to be told. Although much work has been contributed to human trafficking research, this book adds to the extant literature in a number of ways, including a discussion of both labor and sex trafficking, the Midwest as a destination hub for trafficking, police attitudes and responses to trafficking situations, promising practices for service provision to trafficked people, inclusion of LGBTQ people, men, and boys, and the collaboration between legal actors and social service providers.

In the past decade, there has been an overwhelming number of articles and books that have been published on human trafficking, much of which has focused on Southern and/or Border States (Hopper, 2004; Reid, 2010; Busch Armendariz, 2009; Heil, 2012; Ulibarri et al., 2014) or large cities (Raphael, 2008; Raphael & Myers Powell, 2010; Smith, Vardaman, & Snow, 2009; Martin & Pierce, 2014). Although there has been research conducted in the Midwest, the geographic locations have generally been specific to one city (Smith et al., 2009; Williamson & Prior, 2009; Raphael, 2008; Raphael & Myers Powell, 2010; Oselin, 2014; Wilson & Dalton, 2008). We have made efforts to not only focus on St. Louis, but also the nearby counties and the Southern agricultural communities in both Missouri and Illinois. Due to the mobility and fluidity of human trafficking, we felt it important to connect with those most involved in the anti-trafficking efforts throughout the bi-state area. Additionally, much of the research that has been done in the Midwest has generally focused on sex trafficking (Nichols & Heil, 2014; Smith et. al., 2009; Williamson & Prior, 2009; Wilson & Dalton, 2008; Raphael, 2008; Raphael & Myers Powell, 2010; Martin & Pierce, 2014). Focusing research solely on sex trafficking not only underscores the prevalence of labor trafficking in the United States, but also directly impacts the formation of anti-trafficking laws and policies. Therefore, this book not only adds to the literature geographically, but it also emphasizes the realities of both sex trafficking and labor trafficking in the United States.

Beyond location and identified forms of human trafficking, we did not focus our research efforts on just one side of the anti-trafficking movement. Rather, we included the voices of local and federal level law enforcement officials, prosecutors, social service providers, and survivors, providing a triangulation of views. In order to truly understand the anti-trafficking efforts that are being made in St. Louis and the bi-state area, we felt it important to not concentrate our research solely on the work of one set of anti-trafficking advocates, but rather to combine the voices and provide a complete discussion of efforts that are being taken in St. Louis and the bi-state area to combat trafficking. Additionally, we emphasize importance of collaboration between all parties involved. We found that collaboration was central to identifying and protecting victims while punishing offenders. Thus, this book implicates the necessity of collaborating with the various perspectives involved in combatting human trafficking throughout the United States.

Use of Terms

We use the terms "survivor" and "victim" interchangeably throughout the book, recognizing that use of language is a contentious area of debate. Social service providers and advocates generally tend to prefer the term "survivor," as it is viewed as acknowledging the agency, survival, and strength of trafficked people, while "victim" is perceived by some to deny agency to those who have experienced trafficking, by presenting trafficked people as the passive recipients of victimization. At the same time, "survivor" may be viewed by others as minimizing the victimization that trafficked people experience, which may include a broad array of abuses, such as sexual, physical, economic, and psychological abuses, as well as coercive control. "Victim" calls attention to the serious nature of the various abuses that such individuals experience. Professionals in the justice system tend to prefer the term "victim," as this is the legal terminology used in police reports, court reports, and the like. Respondents in this study used the terms interchangeably, including survivors, social service providers, and justice system professionals. We believe these arguments all have merit, and considering the wide audience for this book, use the terms "trafficked people," "victims," and "survivors" interchangeably to represent this spectrum, and also to represent the words and views of the respondents, including survivors, in this study.

We are also sensitive to using the language of modern day slavery to refer to trafficked people. This is a point of contention among some academics, and even the authors have competing views about the use of the term and its applications. In the case of sex trafficking, framing trafficked people as modern slaves may be problematic for a number of reasons. First, sex trafficked individuals in the United States rarely identify themselves as slaves. None of the sex trafficking survivors interviewed for this book identified themselves as slaves. Ostensibly, it is important to frame the issue in the way survivors would themselves. Second, sex trafficking is not at all modern; rather, the way various forms of prostitution are framed is a relatively modern invention. For example, what used to be called juvenile prostitution, as well as prostitution of adults induced by force, fraud, or coercion is now being labeled as sex trafficking. Prostitution under such conditions has perhaps always existed; rather, it is our understandings of sex trafficking that have advanced in the modern day. Third, the slavery rhetoric may also work to mischaracterize the issue, particularly in the context of sex trafficking in the St. Louis bi-state area. As stated by Hoyle, Bosworth, and Dempsey (2011) "By creating 'ideal types' of trafficked women ... the language of slavery oversimplifies our understanding of the range of causes and experiences of trafficking (p.3)." The majority of sex trafficking uncovered in the St. Louis area takes the form of survival sex or functions as an extension of intimate partner violence. The bonds of an individual to a trafficking situation are often economic and psychological in nature. The slavery discourse is typically accompanied by images of girls in chains, handcuffs, or other such signs of physical restraint. In working to educate the public with the goal of increasing identification through citizen tips, this imagery is perhaps counterproductive in its inaccuracy. Such images may be put forth to draw attention to the issue, or perhaps the chains are used to symbolize the economic and psychological binding to a trafficker. Yet, such representations of sex trafficking, conflated with images of bound slaves, may result in misunderstandings of the typical cases of sex trafficking in its oversimplification of the realities of sex trafficking and its multifaceted forms. In addition, such representations may also depict a racist image, as the vast majority of such images depict bonded white girls. African American women and girls are disproportionately represented in crime statistics as trafficking victims, composing 40% of those trafficked, while African Americans make up only 13% of the population, and African American women and girls compose just over half of this percentage. In a thorough search of anti-trafficking materials, few images of Black individuals, among hundreds of images, were found (see Nichols, 2015). This imagery reeks of the "not in my backyard" motif, appealing to the white public to be concerned with sex trafficking if it includes white girls from suburban neighborhoods, accompanied by the public discourse imbuing the resurgence of the "white slave" trade (Doezema, 2005). Moreover, "the language of slavery sets up a false dichotomy between 'ideal victims' who are viewed as exercising no agency and real victims, whose experiences are typically far more nuanced and complicated" (Hoyle, Bosworth, and Dempsey, p. 15). Further, such notions may lead the ideologies of "rescuing" the "slaves," and as the reader will see, "rescue" is not typically the response needed. In addition, sex trafficked individuals in the St. Louis bi-state area typically have freedom of movement, some level of (socially conditioned) choice and agency, and sex trafficking is not supported by U.S. legal systems. This makes it quite distinct from the experiences of African Americans in the U.S. slave trade, which the second author believes is minimized by the slavery rhetoric used in the anti-trafficking movement in its appropriation of the term. Hoyle et al. (2011) note that the symbolism of the slavery rhetoric holds different meanings in different sites, in part depending upon whether a nation has a history of slave-trade. Consequently, the second author prefers not to use the terms slave or modern-day slavery to describe sex trafficking and sex trafficking survivors. Opposing arguments, of which the second author recognizes the merits, hold that bonds to traffickers, whether physical, emotional, or financial, hold sex-trafficked people in virtual captivity, and consequently represent another form of slavery. While acknowledging and agreeing with these views on some level, the second author believes the potential challenges of this terminology outweigh the benefits, regardless of their accuracy. Mischaracterization of the issue and potential infringement on identification trump philosophical notions for this author.

At the same time, in the context of labor trafficking, dynamics of debt bondage and economic exploitation are reminiscent of conditions in the United States that mimicked slavery following emancipation. Freed slaves had little opportunity for advancement, and many rented land, seed, and equipment from former slave owners. Debt often exceeded profit in such circumstances, and kept sharecroppers contractually "stuck" working for white landowners. This bonded labor has been identified by groups such as Anti-Slavery International as equating slavery; it is another form of slavery varying from traditional notions of chattel slavery. Because of the nature of the exploitation of migrant workers in this study, the first author uses the terms slavery and modern-day slavery. Counterarguments hold that debt bondage and economic exploitation are distinct from and minimize the hundreds of years of chattel slavery experienced by African Americans in U.S. history, who were bought and sold at auctions, separated from family members by force, severely beaten, and returned to slave owners when caught attempting escape, all under a legal system that legitimized their status as inferior, denied of agency and humanity in multiple contexts. While the first author acknowledges the distinct nature of the experiences of African Americans in the U.S. slave trade, she believes the potential benefits of this terminology outweigh the challenges, by drawing attention to the exploitive and victimizing nature of labor trafficking, which denies agency and dehumanizes labor trafficked people in the form of a "new" or "modern-day" slavery. The first author holds that there are multiple forms and layers to slavery, and one is not minimized by the presence of another.

Methods

Study Setting

The study setting examines the St. Louis bi-state area based upon federal districts, including the Eastern District of Missouri and the Southwestern District of Illinois. Using the federal districts provided clarity and convenience in examining prosecuted cases, as well as the relationship between federal, state, and county-level prosecution. The districts also coincided with areas of specific interest to the researchers. We were interested in studying the bi-state area, as southern Missouri and southeastern Illinois were identified as spots where agricultural forms of labor trafficking or related violations were occurring, and the St. Louis metro area was identified as a region where both sex and labor trafficking were occurring. St. Louis was initially chosen as a study site, because it was identified by the U.S. Department of Justice as city with increased risk factors, as discussed in relationship to prevalence above (U.S. Department of Justice, 2006, p. 35). St. Louis is viewed as a city with an increased risk for human trafficking, due to its large number of runaways, high drop-out and truancy rates, and large homeless youth population. In addition, while the relationship is unclear, St. Louis is also home to a growing immigrant population, which may be at increased risk due to St. Louis's high rates of ethnic/racial residential segregation and insular communities, as well as vulnerability due to refugee status and/or economic marginalization. Immigrants from Bosnia, Vietnam, Burundi, Uganda, Iraq, and Syria have entered the area at various points over the last two decades, and may be at risk of labor or sex trafficking. In surrounding agricultural communities, throughout southeastern Missouri and southwestern Illinois, migrant labor is burgeoning. Migrant labor is needed, as farmers look for inexpensive labor, in fields and orchards, as well as food processing factories.

Further, a thriving sex trade industry is present on the east side. The Metro St. Louis area has also been identified as the top city in the nation for strip clubs per capita; strip clubs have been found to be an underground venue for trafficking (Proud, 2013). Moreover, large convention centers and multiple sporting venues are present in the St. Louis metropolitan area, and have been identified as potential sources of buyers. St. Louis is home to the St. Louis Blues hockey team, the St. Louis Cardinals baseball team, and the Rams football team, drawing hundreds of thousands of visitors each year. The St. Louis convention center, The America's

Center, also draws hundreds of thousands of visitors annually. Further, a large convention center in Collinsville, IL, The Gateway Center, located less than fifteen miles from downtown St. Louis, holds approximately six hundred events annually, attracting tens of thousands of visitors each year. Research indicates that drawing large groups, particularly large groups of men, may potentially increase sex trafficking due to the increased demand for sex-for-sale. Traffickers may take advantage of this increased opportunity for profitability. In addition, the presence of a large airport increases the risk of trafficking in the city, as traffickers have been known to sell women and girls to customers moving in and out of airports, who are staying in hotels nearby for business trips. St. Louis's centralized location at the crossroads of major cross country interstates makes the movement of victims through the area more likely (The Covering House, 2013). Interstate 55, I-44, I-70, and I-64 run through St. Louis, and are also major "connector" interstates as well. Compared to other large cities, this centralized location, combined with the larger number of interstates, produces increased risk for placement on the "circuit." For example, I-55 north goes straight to Chicago, and I-55 south moves straight to Memphis, with connecting interstates to Nashville and Atlanta. Interstate 44 connects to Oklahoma City, with connections to 35 south, which then proceeds to Dallas. Further, I-70 goes straight west to Kansas City, with connections to I-35, which then moves north to Minneapolis. I-70 also connects at Kansas City with I-29, which goes to Omaha. Interstate 70 also goes east to Indianapolis. In prosecuted cases in the St. Louis area, Chicago, Minneapolis, Omaha, Kansas City, Indianapolis, Atlanta, and Dallas have all been implicated as cities falling on various "circuits" of traffickers. Traffickers are known to take victims on interstate "circuits" and the geographic location makes St. Louis more likely to fall on the "circuit" (The Covering House, 2013; Nichols & Heil, 2014; Williamson & Prior, 2009). In addition, St. Louis is one of relatively few cities, 42 in all, with an anti-trafficking task force and local coalition composed of various community partners in the justice system and social services (Moossy, 2009). The area is home

to an anti-trafficking movement, with coalitions throughout the
two federal districts.

Sampling

The sample includes a total of thirty-one respondents, including
survivors, social service providers, and justice system professionals.
Individuals were recruited based upon their recognized work with
human trafficking victims, and/or their experiences as trafficking
survivors. The sample was derived from a small member-list of
anti-trafficking organizations in St. Louis, and snowball sampling
from these sources. Survivors of sex trafficking (n=4) who participated were also social service providers. Social service providers
(n=14) worked in a variety of different areas, which often overlapped. This included children's services, foster care, direct services
for trafficking survivors, and education and outreach. Justice system professionals (n=17) included police officers in multiple jurisdictions throughout the bi-state area, legal services attorneys, a
former federal prosecutor, professionals in the juvenile division of
the family courts, and legal advocates (who could also be viewed
as social service providers, n=5). Respondents were generally eager
to participate, and provide additional referrals. Four individuals
who were asked to participate did not participate, initially expressing interest, but who did not follow through. This includes two
prosecutors, an FBI investigator, and a U.S. Representative from
Missouri involved in drafting anti-trafficking legislation.

In total, representatives from sixteen organizations took part in
the study, including the St. Louis Police Department, the U.S. Attorney's Office, the Covering House, the International Institute,
Legal Services of Eastern Missouri, the St. Louis County Police,
Madison County Sheriff's Department, Roxana Police, the Juvenile
Division of the Family Courts in St. Louis, Magdalene House, Rescue and Restore St. Louis (which branched out into The Coalition
Against Trafficking and Exploitation, CATE, shortly after the research was conducted for this book), Rescue and Restore Southwestern Illinois, and representatives from four organizations who
wished for their organizations' names to remain confidential. In-

dividuals were chosen for the sample because of their direct and in-depth involvement with trafficking victims and cases, provision of trainings, or presence on anti-trafficking task forces or coalitions. Participants were recruited by individually contacting each potential respondent by email, in some cases with a follow up phone call.

Data Collection

Data were collected in two phases. The first phase of the research involved a pilot study conducted in 2011, including twelve participants in face-to-face interviews and focus groups, as well as participant observation in trainings and coalition meetings. Both researchers were open about their status as professors and researchers of human trafficking. Field notes were taken at the trainings. The interviews and focus groups took place at individual offices, and in one case, at a convenient coffee shop. The interviews lasted approximately 45 minutes to an hour. The focus group interviews and individual interviews were audio-recorded and transcribed word-for-word by the researchers. All quotes that appear in this book are presented exactly as respondents stated them. Based upon the results of the pilot study (the results appear in Nichols & Heil, 2014), we conducted a second wave of data collection in 2013–2014, interviewing another nineteen respondents. Interviews in the second wave of research also typically lasted approximately 45 minutes to one hour, and took place in private offices, and in one case a convenient and quiet coffee shop. The interviews were face-to-face, except for two interviews which were conducted over the phone, which were also recorded and transcribed word-for-word. A semi-structured interview guide was used, developed based upon themes uncovered in the first-phase pilot study, but other themes and threads were encouraged in the open conversations with the respondents to allow for important information to come out that we had not considered. Interviews typically concluded with the question, "Is there anything I didn't ask you that you wish I would have asked you?" This allowed for themes to develop that did not initially consider. All interviews were audio-recorded and transcribed by the researchers, a research assistant, and a professional transcriptionist. The transcriptions were rechecked for accuracy by both the authors. Participant observation at trainings and meetings was also conducted, with field notes taken and recorded for later reference. Organizations also eagerly offered access to training materials, informational handouts, meeting minutes, programmatic design materials, and more. In addition to interview data, field notes, and organization-provided materials, court reports were also used to examine prosecuted cases of sex and labor trafficking, as well as those cases falling under related charges.

Data Analysis

The transcribed interviews were first selectively coded according to the study design and interview guide. Themes related to social services, law enforcement, sex trafficking, and labor trafficking were initially selectively coded and labeled by hand, and additionally coded to label overlapping areas. After selectively coding the transcripts for these core categories, merged narrative accounts for each core category were created as separate files, which were then open-coded by hand in order to label and pull out recurring patterns and themes within each core category. For example, the core category of sex trafficking included types of sex trafficking, risk factors, and sex trafficking techniques. Additional subthemes were further identified within these categories through taxonomic analysis. Taxonomic analysis was used to label additional "types" or subthemes of the core categories. For example, "types" of sex trafficking techniques included traffickers' use of recruitment practices, placing barriers to leaving a trafficking situation, and ways of conducting trafficking operations, such as interstate movement and use of the Internet. Negative cases were also explored, in order to ensure the accuracy of the data analysis and to avoid any potential bias. Initial coding processes were checked and discussed by the authors, to establish reliability. Member-checking was also used for selected Chapters, 3, 5, and 6 to ensure the accuracy of the presentation and interpretation of the data. Member checking includes review of written work by research participants; four research participants volunteered to read the written analysis with no discrepancies reported.

Chapter Overviews

The book is divided into two main themes: types of trafficking and responses to human trafficking. Chapters Two and Three specifically focus on the types of human trafficking identified in St. Louis and the bi-state area, while Chapters Four, Five, and Six focus on the responses to human trafficking. The book concludes with implications for law enforcement and social services, and recommendations for the future in combating human trafficking in St. Louis and the bi-state area.

Chapter Two explores labor trafficking in the St. Louis bi-state area. The chapter begins with a discussion of how labor trafficking is often overlooked by advocates, law enforcement officials, and policy makers. However, despite this neglect, victims of labor trafficking are trapped in systems of involuntary servitude and debt bondage with little to no pay. This section is followed by a discussion of labor trafficking laws and the types of labor trafficking that have been identified in St. Louis and the bi-state area. The chapter is then divided into a dichotomy of labor trafficking based on geographic location. The first part of the divide discusses labor trafficking in the agricultural communities of Southern Missouri and Southern Illinois. In these regions, traffickers use bait and switch techniques to bring in migrating laborers who find themselves economically and physically trapped in isolated communities. Most of these migrant laborers are foreign nationals who live under a constant fear of deportation; a tool of control and intimidation for the trafficker. The chapter then shifts the discussion of labor trafficking to the other geographic divide identified in the city of St. Louis. Most of the identified labor trafficking in St. Louis has been in the industrial sector, thereby creating profiles of both the victim and trafficker that are unique from the agricultural communities. This dichotomous relationship results in differing prosecutions and misidentification, specifically with visa and workplace violations.

Chapter Three examines dynamics of sex trafficking in the St. Louis bi-state area. The chapter opens with a discussion of the multifaceted backgrounds of survivors, as well as typical and atypical cases of sex trafficking, then relates the research findings to contemporary characterizations of sex trafficking and the importance of recognizing the broad spectrum of sex trafficking experiences. This section is followed by an investigation of the types of sex trafficking occurring in the region, including pimp-controlled prostitution, survival sex, false-front trafficking schemes, familial trafficking, and child pornography-as-trafficking. Next, risk factors related to structural inequality, weak social institutions, and lack of social safety nets are explored. Specifically, poverty, truancy, drop-out status, and runaway or throwaway status, coupled with lack of related resources are examined. Economic and racial marginalization, and marginalization based upon sexual orientation are also discussed in this section. Last, sex trafficking techniques, including recruitment, barriers to leaving, and trafficking operations are explored.

Chapter Four focuses on the legal response to human trafficking by law enforcement officials and prosecutors. The chapter begins with the general challenges associated with policing human trafficking. The discussion then focuses on specific training techniques for local and federal level officers, and the officers' perceptions of the trainings. Officers varied on their perceptions of the training, but most felt that in order to be better trained in identifying and protecting victims while punishing the offenders, the trainings required an overhaul that would better suit the needs of law enforcement officials. Following this is a discussion of how officers perceive human trafficking in St. Louis and the bi-state area. The perceptions of human trafficking were generally based on the investigative techniques that were used by officers. Each technique of investigation was challenging, but with new legislation, online investigations have proven to be the most challenging. Additionally, with regards to investigation, labor trafficking and sex trafficking were investigated much differently. Given the neglect of much of the labor trafficking cases, those cases that had been identified required resourceful techniques by advocates, officers, and prosecutors. Next the chapter discusses the various avenues of human trafficking investigations both at the local level and federal level. The chapter concludes with the challenges that arise when prosecuting a potential human trafficking case.

Chapter Five begins by examining the work of social service and advocacy organizations in their efforts towards increasing the identification of trafficked people. Specifically, community awareness, direct outreach, education and training, and collaboration are explored. The chapter begins by investigating education and awareness campaigns, with the goal of increasing tips and reports by ordinary citizens. Next, training of professionals in the social services, healthcare, and justice system sectors are examined. In addition, training of others likely to come into contact with trafficked people such as hotel staff, cable company employees, and postal workers are described. Further, informal and formal channels of collaboration are explored between community organizations. The chapter concludes by illustrating remaining gaps in training, collaboration, and direct outreach identified by the respondents, and the efforts of local organizations to address them.

Chapter Six explicitly examines service provision to sex trafficked or commercially sexually exploited people. The chapter illustrates the need for sex-trafficking-specific services, highlighting the unique trauma that sex trafficking survivors experience. Next, the limitations and challenges of available responses, such as foster care placements, juvenile detention, residential and rehabilitation placements are delineated, simultaneously examining why girls may run away from services. Further, survivor-led, survivor-informed, and survivor-defined services are also examined. Last, gaps in services, such as lack of shelter, housing, and services are investigated, highlighting that the demand for services exceeds the availability of services. This is true for women and girls, and heightened for adults, boys, and LGBTQ people. Chapter Seven concludes this book, emphasizing the implications of the research findings for social service providers and law enforcement in the areas of both labor and sex trafficking. The importance of ongoing education and training to social service providers, law enforcement, and front line workers, as well as the necessary funding to support it, is highlighted. Moreover, education and training provided to social services and law enforcement in cultural competency, related to providing assistance to LGBTQ trafficked or sexually exploited people, as well as migrant labor-trafficked people, is recommended. Further, increased availability of services, particularly shelter/housing, survivor-defined and trauma-informed care is recommended. Additionally, in terms of sex trafficking, sex-trafficking-specific services and survivor-involved programming are implicated. The chapter closes with policy recommendations and projections for the future of the anti-trafficking movement.

Chapter 2

Labor Trafficking

Hidden behind concrete walls or disappearing into the vast orchards of the Midwest, labor trafficking is one of the most misun-
derstood and misidentified forms of human trafficking in St. Louis
and the bi-state area. As noted in Chapter One, human trafficking
is an umbrella term for various forms of victimization and exploitation. Many times labor trafficking is viewed as a related immigration
offense or traffickers are charged with wage per hour or visa violations. Through the course of investigating and interviewing for this
project, police stated they are not investigating labor trafficking
cases; policy makers have openly confessed that they are not considering the victims of labor trafficking when writing new legislation
intended to protect victims of human trafficking. Social service
providers that are making attempts to protect identified victims of
labor trafficking have argued that their resources are limited, thereby
reducing their ability to identify and protect victims of labor trafficking. Socially and politically, the term human trafficking has become synonymous with sex trafficking, leaving the victims of labor
trafficking virtually invisible. The purpose of this chapter is to identify labor trafficking in its various forms as identified in St. Louis
and the bi-state area. Additionally, we will discuss what measures
are being made to protect victims of labor trafficking. In spite of the
efforts being made, the political and social obstacles are nearly impossible to overcome as the victims of labor trafficking slowly dis-
appear into a reality of forced labor, little to no pay, and into a system that can only be described as modern-day slavery.

Before any discussion of labor trafficking in St. Louis and the
bi-state area, we will first address the general definitional
problems. The Trafficking Victims Protection Act of 2000 (TVPA)
defines labor trafficking as: "The recruitment, harboring, trans-

portation, provision, or obtaining of a person for labor or services, through the use of force, fraud or coercion for the purpose of subjection to involuntary servitude, peonage, debt bondage or slavery." For the purposes of this chapter, we will be using the federal definition of labor trafficking due to the fact that the cases in St. Louis and the bi-state area are more likely to be prosecuted at the federal level in association to related immigration offenses. Included in the definition of labor trafficking are the various types, which are bonded labor (debt bondage), forced labor, and child labor. Advocates have stated that each of these types of labor trafficking have been identified in the bi-state area, but are not necessarily prosecuted as such.

Beyond the scope of definitions and forms of labor trafficking are the locations at which labor trafficking occurs. Labor trafficking has been identified in restaurants, factories, in orchards and fields, hair salons, lawn care and construction companies. There are so many avenues of labor trafficking that it becomes overwhelming to attempt to explain or define the various forms of oppression and exploitation. Therefore, for the purposes of this chapter, we are not going to identify every form of labor trafficking evident in the bi-state area, but rather discuss the possibilities for labor trafficking based on those cases that have been identified. The complexities and interwoven challenges of identification are significant, and it is our purpose to bring out of the shadows a comprehensive discussion of labor trafficking in its many forms evident in St. Louis and the bi-state area.

Geographically, labor trafficking is identified and perceived much differently between St. Louis and the neighboring communities. Because of this diversity, we will discuss labor trafficking in a geographical context, beginning with the outside rural areas in which labor trafficking has been identified in orchards, restaurants, and factories.

Labor Trafficking in the Rural Communities of the Bi-State Region

Traveling into the southern regions of both Illinois and Missouri, the landscape shifts from metropolitan buildings to fields and orchards ready for the harvest of peaches, pumpkins, corn, and melons. Makeshift fruit stands sit on the sides of the roads and every twenty miles or so, another industrial farm vandalizes the landscape. It is here that men and women from Michoacán, Oaxaca, or Puebla, Mexico migrate to between the months of February and December looking for menial work in the agricultural sector. Others travel from Guatemala, El Salvador, and Haiti. Within the borders of the United States, migrant families travel from Florida and Texas looking for ways to provide for their children. The diversity of the people is as diverse as the jobs that are available for menial, migrant work. From pruning peaches to cotton gin processing, and from tomatoes and watermelons to chicken factories, migrant workers come to these rural communities eager to find work in order to continue their survival in the United States. Often times the migrant workers are fraudulently led to believe that they will be working in construction or other higher paying jobs, but find themselves stranded working in restaurants. Because of a vulnerable status related to immigration status and language barriers, many of the migrant workers find themselves in an impossible situation of debt bondage and/or paper holding, leaving them with no other option but to continue to work for little or no pay under inhumane working and living conditions.

Our research took us to the southernmost regions of Missouri and Illinois, and there we found only a handful of individuals working with the migrant community and exposing some of the potential cases of labor trafficking. The cases they witnessed were most closely associated with debt bondage and forced labor. We saw no evidence of child labor, but that is not to say that it does not exist in these regions of the Midwest. In fact, it was eluded to that some migrant children may use their summer free time working in the cotton fields. As was stated by one advocate when discussing the importance of outreach to every member of the migrant community, "[if] you don't let me out to go talk to the parents, the parents aren't gonna let their kids come in here and sign up for [the] summer youth program when they can have them out there chopping cotton." Again, we found no evidence that these children are underage and are forced to work in the fields. Additionally, advocates who have had contact with the children of migrants indicate that the children are usually U.S. citizens receiving some form of public assistance, yet their parents are undocumented. Therefore, children are not only being monitored by their parents, but also by the state, which maintains surveillance over truancy and labor laws. This is not to say that it is not possible for child labor to occur in the rural communities of Illinois and Missouri, but it is an issue that may warrant future research. Thus, given no concrete evidence of child labor, we only focused our attention on the men and women who have been forced to labor in a system of debt bondage.

The key concern of the advocates interviewed for this project regarding labor trafficking is forced agricultural labor, specifically the holding of personal identifying papers and debt bondage. The particular concern for one advocate was the crew leaders, or those who are responsible for hiring, managing, and organizing the field workers. According to the advocate, "some of the workers are having to pay to get their job, so they're in debt up front before they ever touch foot to the fields.... [It costs them] from two hundred to five hundred dollars for them to get the job." In other words, because the jobs are relatively scarce, crew leaders offer jobs to those migrant workers who are willing to pay the crew leader money under the table to have a position in the field. And what if the migrant worker does not have the money up front? According to the advocate, "[the crew leaders] deduct it [from their pay] ... and then they can't leave [the farm] because they are obligated to pay back." Although a subtle process, the cycle of debt bondage begins. The migrant worker is now attached to the farm, forced to work for the crew leader until his/her payment for the job is covered. This can become incredibly difficult given the minimal pay many of the migrant laborers are receiving.

The system of debt bondage was found to be more common with the crew leaders asking for money up front in order to obtain employment. However, there have been identified cases in which the contractor or boss is holding pay from the workers. This is even the case if the worker is not in some sort of up front debt due to job placement. One case that is, at the time of this writing, currently being pursued by advocates was explained as:

> [There] is this lady that wants to come and talk with me. I don't think she will, but I'm going to try. She's undocumented. Her husband is undocumented. They're working on a chicken farm through a contractor. Their little boy is a U.S. citizen, and he has a lot of mental disabilities. He's on Medicaid, and she said ... 'We're only getting half our pay. He's only giving us half our paycheck, but what can we do about it? We're undocumented. And we have to take what he gives us. But who are we going to complain to? And where else are we going to work? And he's been charging us to fill out the paperwork that we have to have to continue my little boy's Medicaid and medical benefits. And he's charging us for it.' And she said he'll do it on his own good time whenever he gets ready. And she said, 'I can't go to anybody because ... we're gonna lose our jobs. We're gonna be deported. My little boy won't have any medical care at all in Mexico.'

This case scenario not only highlights the holding of pay, but also the immense fear that the migrants feel. It is that fear that keeps them from reporting the abuse, both financial and psychological. There exists a distrust of law enforcement, and a real fear of being deported. The migrant community is an isolated community. According to a social service provider: " ... if they are coming in on a bus ... they are going to be stranded. Where are they going to go? How are they going to get home? Where are they going to work?" Just for the need of survival, many of the migrant workers have succumbed to their abuse because the alternative (e.g. deportation, arrest, loss of family, etc.) is unthinkable.

Using subtle techniques of psychological control, many times the migrant workers do not question the current situation. One local advocate described a situation of a young Hispanic woman working at a Chinese restaurant who had found a trailer she wanted to rent for $250 a month. She had come to the advocate asking for interpretation services as her English was limited. Therefore, the advocate went with the woman and explained the situation as follows:

> It was out in the country in this area. And it just so happened that I knew the landlady. So I went out there with her, and ... the Hispanic lady said, 'Well yeah, I love the trailer. Can you tell her I want it?' And I said sure. She said, well ... 'I'll need to call my manager to bring me the money.' And I said, oh, so today is payday? And she said, 'No, she always keeps my money.' And I'm like, for this month? 'No, she's always kept my money. I have to ask her when I want something and then she'll give me the money when I tell her what I am going to do with the money.'... So the lady came out there, and this was a Chinese restaurant, and she came out there, and she gave her the money and I thought, well, she's gonna at least be out from under her wing and have a place to stay.

Again, this case illustrates that her money was not only being held, but also controlled by her manager at the restaurant. Unfortunately, the advocate was only able to help at this point in the process. As she expressed, she believed that the migrant worker was getting out of a controlled situation. However, six months later, the advocate ran into a crew leader that worked for the landlady renting the trailer to the Hispanic woman. The advocate decided to follow up on the situation, asking the crew leader if he knew how she was doing. According to the crew leader, the Hispanic lady was in the trailer for a month and " ... the lady from the Chinese restaurant come [sic] picked her back up, took her back up there to live with her, and she was cleaning house at night and doing all of her chores for the manager, plus working in the restaurant during the day." As with the other cases, this change in her living situation was not reported, and she was once again trapped under the control of her manager.

Managers and crew leaders do not only control through the holding of pay. Other times, the immigration papers of the migrant laborers will be held until the debt to the crew leader or manager is repaid. One social service provider explained to us a case she worked in the early 1990s that still resonated with her:

> ... There were about three to four hundred people from Oaxaca, Mexico, and they were out in the middle of a cornfield in the middle of nowhere ... They said all of their papers were being held. And when I went out to the field, they were all wearing badges with a number and nobody had a name. But they had a picture ID with a number ... And ... the farmer up there [had a big sign]: 'Trespassers will be shot,' with a big pistol ... so people were very apprehensive. And the people had no way to even get to town, you know, they were totally dependent ... they told me that their papers ... all of their documents were being held until they finished in the fields.

More recently, there has been a case of a woman who had escaped from a crew leader who was holding her papers, but she was still living within close vicinity of him. According to a social service provider, "[the crew leader] had threatened her. He had physically harmed one of the other women in the crew who was taken to the emergency room. She was terrified. She said he had her documents." The facts of this case were eventually relayed to Immigration Customs and Enforcement, but the social service provider had since lost track of her. Unfortunately, that is the case for most of the migrant workers. Due to their migration patterns, once identified, they often return to their country of origin, migrate to another community, and advocates lose track of them completely.

Aside from debt bondage and psychological control, migrant workers also have to consider how to afford the basic necessities for themselves and their families in spite of their existing debt. This is especially true for housing. Housing in the rural agricultural communities we investigated is extremely limited. As was conveyed to us by one advocate, housing for rooted community members alone is difficult to find, and for an undocumented migrant living in a strange land with limited knowledge of the language, he/she becomes dependent on crew leaders or bosses to find housing. In many cases, there is a "bait and switch" occurring, adding yet another layer of exploitation. For example:

> [They was a couple that] came in with a crew from Florida ... They were promised they would be paid $300 a week to pitch melons. They weren't ... They were told that [a] hotel room would be paid for, and they were [then] left stranded and [only] had one night in the hotel ...

This case had a happy ending as advocates were able to provide rent assistance, as well as connect the couple with another crew leader who was able to provide paid work. Other migrant workers have not been so lucky as to find assistance.

> I hear ... where [the migrant workers are] left stranded or they were made promises that they would be given housing, and then that's taken out of their check. 'Oh, well, we're not making the money we thought so ... we're gonna take out for the hotel. And, oh well, you know the meals ... the water ...' and before you know it, [the migrant workers] are working for nothing out there. And they're not gonna leave, because they're bound and they owe, and a lot of them, where are they going to go?

Unfortunately, this scenario is much too common for the migrant laborers in the rural communities. Without the ability to find assistance, they are left stranded and forced to work under a situation of debt bondage.

Many times, the housing debt is not owed to the crew leader, but rather to a landlord who has learned to capitalize off of the vulnerabilities associated with the illegal status of the migrant laborers. Landlords are able to charge up to fifteen times what local residents would pay. According to a local source, "they can get $50 a head for over four in the family—that's what they ... pay per week ... They will make substandard run down deteriorating trailers available at about $800–900 a month rent." Substandard is a polite word for some of the living conditions the migrant workers face. One migrant worker who had complained about his housing situation to a local advocate described his living condition as follows:

> ... The holes are so big in the walls that rats are getting
> in the walls and they are dancing at night keeping me
> awake ... I told the landlord, and ... you know what he
> did? He gave me some Walmart baggies and a thing of ...
> caulking. He gave me a caulking gun with two tubes of
> caulking and Walmart bags. And he said, 'that's the rem-
> edy to the mice in the wall!'

Other workers have been found sleeping on porches, empty stores,
abandoned buildings and other places not suitable for sleeping because they are unable to afford the high rental rates inflated by
landlords or the general hotel cost. This is simply because the pay
is being held, or they are not being paid at all.

It must be clarified that not all of the migrant workers are undocumented. Some of them are legally in the United States on
work visas, yet due to language barriers and lack of education,
they still find themselves in a trafficking situation. For example,
a young man from Texas found himself stranded after being laid
off from construction work. According to a social service
provider:

> He and his buddy ... were told that they ... would be ...
> making $400 in [a] Chinese restaurant, and they would
> have a place to stay, and ... they could do the buddy plan
> like they wanted. [A temp hiring service] gave them a
> number to call if they didn't like the restaurant or had a
> problem. They would pay for them a bus ticket back
> home. And he said what happened was they put them
> on ... vans ... in the middle of the night. His buddy went
> one direction; he was in a van going another direction.
> And they didn't even tell them what town they were going
> to. They had no idea. And they were met by these man-
> agers of the restaurant in the middle of the night, and
> taken, you know, dispersed out to the restaurants ...

This social service provider happened to come across this young
man at a grocery store where he conveyed to her that his current
job and living situation was not what had been promised:

'I'm calling this number and it doesn't work. They said
that they would send me home with a bus ticket, and I'm
working at this Chinese restaurant and they're not paying
me $400 a week. And he's making me recycle food off of
the plates back into the buffet bar. And I'm having to live
with him, and he's mean …'

Fortunately for him, this social service provider was able to use her
resources and get him back on a bus returning to Texas.

This case represents the very simple bait and switch tactics that
are being used by traffickers; promising one job and leaving those
who migrate to the community stranded. Individuals are told they
will be paid a certain salary, and the hourly wage is less than what
they were promised. Housing may be promised but is suddenly de-
ducted from their pay. They are told that they can leave whenever
they want, but they are caught in a cycle of debt bondage unable
to escape. Papers and pay are being held, and workers are being
controlled through economic and psychological manipulation.

Although the tactics of control violate visa and immigration
laws, social service providers and local level law enforcement officials face many problems identifying and working with potential
victims of labor trafficking in rural migrant communities. As was
stated previously, many of the migrant laborers are distrustful of
law enforcement, so it is unlikely that they will approach any person with a badge even if they believe that they are being victimized.
Beyond that general distrust are additional problems in identifying
and protecting victims of labor trafficking in the rural communities. The first of these is the immense isolation. As has been stated,
and will be discussed in other chapters, victims of sex trafficking
are sold over and over again. Therefore, there is an opportunity to
identify the victims of sex trafficking as they are being advertised
for potential buyers. With labor trafficking, on the other hand,
they come in on a bus, go to the crew leader or manager, and that
is it. There is only one contact, and no real opportunity to identify
who is a victim of trafficking beyond outreach.

Unfortunately, even through outreach, there exists another underlying problem specific to agricultural laborers: no one is really

sure who is actually working in the fields. An advocate explained this problem when she was attempting to discover if wages were being held from the workers. According to her:

> I've heard for years that money has been taken out of their checks; that they are being charged for jobs, and it makes me so mad; because I know the farmers don't know this ... The farmers don't know what these crew leaders are doing. And the farmers have no idea what the peoples' names are in the field ... [When we ask for income verification], they're like, 'well I don't know who is out there in that field. You're gonna have to come talk to the crew leader.' And half the time, the crew leader doesn't know who's out there in the field. And the people sure don't know who the crew leader is, so even if they wanted to press charges against the crew leader, nine times out of ten all they know is Paco or Gajo, and you know, they don't have a name to associate with them ... They get a nickname and that's all they are going to tell them.

This issue was prevalent amongst many of the rural advocates we interviewed for this project. All you can do is outreach, but it is unlikely that you will get any real information from the migrant workers. The only way to discover if wages or papers are being held is when a migrant worker comes forward, and as already stated, it is rare for a migrant to expose his/her own victimization. As one social service provider described the migrant community, "they're survivors, and I think they'll brush it off and keep going."

Potential victims of labor trafficking in rural communities may also not come forward because of a general fear for their own livelihood. According to one advocate, "The fear doesn't let them complain. They depend on their work. They depend on their jobs. They have a family to take care of, so they don't say anything." Another advocate expressed a similar sentiment:

> I think because of the risk of losing their job, the isolation ... if they are coming in on a bus ... they are going to be stranded. Where are they going to go? How are they

going to get home? Where are they going to work? I think these issues are so big just for survival that they think 'I guess I can live with this. I mean, this is not a good life, but I don't have a choice.'

Finally, legal officials and social service providers have difficulty in identifying and protecting potential victims of labor trafficking in rural communities due to the inherent mobility. The migrant laborers move with the seasonal agricultural work, so they cannot be tracked. Only those that have some sort of roots can truly be identified, for they learn the safe places for social services and protection. Those that are new to the community are generally not aware of these outlets and will most likely stay quiet. Unfortunately, it is those migrants new to the community who need to be identified and protected, for they are the most vulnerable. Regardless of whether or not the migrant laborers have roots in the community, they still follow the work and create their own migrating patterns: "Some live here and move around and then come back.... Others just move around."

The above problems associated with labor trafficking are not unique to the rural communities. In the St. Louis metropolitan area, similar problems exist for those affected by labor trafficking. What is unique about the rural community is the type of labor trafficking that has been identified, specifically agricultural, factory, and restaurant work, as well as the awareness of the prevalence of labor trafficking. In St. Louis and the surrounding communities, the labor trafficking that has been identified looks much different, and the awareness of labor trafficking is much more limited.

Labor Trafficking in St. Louis and the Metro-East

Labor trafficking in St. Louis and the surrounding metropolitan communities is much different from the trafficking situations identified in the rural communities. The first difference is the demographic of the victims in St. Louis and the surrounding communities. As stated, in rural Missouri and rural Illinois, the majority of the victims are of Hispanic descent. However, in St. Louis and the surrounding communities, those victims that have been identified have been from Africa, Latin America, Eastern Europe, and Asia. Therefore, there is a diverse group of potential victims living within localized ethnic communities.

How labor trafficking is perceived in St. Louis and the surrounding communities is also unique compared to the rural areas represented in our research. If any form of labor trafficking is identified, it is not likely that it will be prosecuted as a trafficking case. Given this, almost every individual from St. Louis and the surrounding communities interviewed for this project acknowledged that labor trafficking is "probably" occurring, but it is not being investigated. When asked, "Why is this the case?" The general response was that "it remains so hidden in these ethnic communities ... [W]e face a real challenge in even identifying victims in the first place."

Generally, the victims of labor trafficking that are identified are usually identified in conjunction with sex trafficking or sexual abuse, and it is more likely that the investigation will stop there. For example, in the St. Louis area, there have been identified undocumented workers who find themselves in domestic servitude. According to one social service provider, "It happens in that situation that they're trafficked to be nannies, household servants, and they have no voice, so they get sexually abused too." Given that there is more likely to be evidence for the sexual abuse, prosecutors are more likely pursue a charge that will be successful. Therefore, the labor trafficking part of the situation becomes relatively obsolete.

In other cases, labor trafficking may be occurring, but the employer will be charged with a visa violation. Because labor trafficking is commonly associated with foreign nationals, there are a number of visa violations with which an employer may be charged. As explained by a representative from the Department of Labor, the following are the possible visa violation charges that can be brought forth:

- 18 USC § 1546: Visa Fraud
- 18 USC § 982: Criminal forfeiture in conjunction with 1546
- 18 USC § 1324: Harboring and bringing in aliens

- 18 USC § 1324a: Unlawful employment of aliens
- 18 USC § 1001: False statements
- 18 USC § 1351 : Fraud in foreign labor contracts
- 18 USC § 1589: Forced labor
- 18 USC § 1592: Document servitude (taking a passport)
- 18 USC § 1343: Wire fraud for pay
- 18 USC § 1341 Mail fraud for pay
- 18 USC § 371 Conspiracy

With each of these visa charges are associated violations which include: selling visas, failure to pay minimum wage and prevailing wage as required by the Department of Labor, charging of illegal fees, bait and switch, and benching, which is no pay for waiting to work. As was highlighted earlier, much of the visa violations that are occurring in the rural communities are bait and switch, charging of illegal fees, and failure to pay minimum wage. In St. Louis and the surrounding communities, the cases that potentially could have been a labor trafficking case have been prosecuted as visa violations under one of the above mentioned statutes.

Case Studies

In 2009, Missouri became the first state in which the Racketeer Influenced and Corrupt Organizations Act (RICO) was used to prosecute a trafficking ring. The company that violated this statute was known as Giant Labor Solutions based out of Kansas City, Missouri. Employers promised hundreds of undocumented workers, mostly from the Dominican Republic, Jamaica, and the Philippines, well-paying jobs in the United States. However, "Giant Labor and two other metro-area companies turned the workers into slaves, fanning them out to housekeeping jobs in hotels and other businesses in 14 states while forcing them to live, sometimes eight at a time, in small apartments for which they were charged exorbitant rent ..." (Draper, 2009). The workers paid Giant Labor Solutions thousands of dollars to be brought into the United States, and when they got to the United States, they "were charged so many fees that they were sometimes told on payday they owed the company money" (ibid.). In 2011, Abrorkhodja Askarkhodjaev, the Uzbekistan national who owned Giant Labor Solutions, "pleaded guilty to conspiracy to engage in racketeering, in violation of 18 U.S.C. §1962; fraud in foreign labor contracting, in violation of 18 U.S.C. §§1351 and 1349; identity theft, in violation of 18 U.S.C. §1028; and evasion of corporate employment tax, in violation of 26 U.S.C. §7201. The district court 1 imposed a sentence of 144 months in prison, 3 years of supervised release, and $1,007,492.28 in restitution" (*United States of America v. Abrorkhodja Askarkhodjaev*, 2011). Since 2011, *United States of America v. Abrorkhodja Askarkhodjaev* has been the only case in Missouri tried under the statute, 18 U.S.C. §§1351.

The United States Attorney's Office for the Eastern District of Missouri has recently prosecuted two high profile cases as visa violations which could also be identified as examples of labor trafficking in St. Louis. The first of these is Robert Brake along with his company Brake Landscaping & Lawncare, Inc. In 2009, Robert Brake and his company were charged with "fraudulently obtaining H-2B worker visas to support his landscaping business" (www.justice.gov. a, 2012, accessed June 2014). An H2B visa is a labor visa used to temporarily hire a non-agricultural worker, and is good for approximately ten months.

> Between March 2008 and February 2010, Robert Brake and his company illegally sub-contracted H-2B workers to an associate on a weekly basis at a profit of more than $2 an hour per alien. In order to facilitate illegal year-round employment of temporary H-2B visa workers, Brake Landscaping employees were hired by another company owned by Robert Brake, Brake Snow and Ice Removal, artificially creating a need for temporary or seasonal workers that didn't actually exist (ibid.).

Robert Brake pleaded guilty to "a misdemeanor charge of employing illegal aliens," and Brake Landscaping & Lawncare, Inc. "pled guilty to one felony count of conspiracy to commit visa fraud" (ibid.). Both were sentenced to two years of probation.

In 2012, J & J Industrial Supply, Inc. "knowingly hired illegal workers and circumvented ... immigration laws for financial gain" (www.justice.gov b, 2012, accessed June 2014). The company had "knowingly and intentionally [hired] more than 10 illegal aliens in a 12-month period," and "by utilizing these aliens realized proceeds of approximately $150,000 during the time of the offense" (ibid.). The company received one year probation for the offense, as well as agreed to "forfeit $150,000 and a 2011 Toyota Highlander used in facilitating the illegal activity" (ibid.).

Two other Missouri cases described by a representative from the Department of Labor included a China buffet that had allegations of trafficking because of pay roll deductions and no overtime. The employers of the China buffet were sentenced to six months incarceration, and six months house arrest. There was also a case of a landscaping business that made a profit from housing fees and uniforms. In the case of the landscaping business, employers were charging workers $110 bi-weekly per worker living in housing owned by the company. There were approximately 35–40 workers per unit, and the employers had installed video cameras at the door to control the movement of the workers. The employers were charged and sentenced to 180 days of confinement plus $120,000 payment in restitution.

Identifying and Prosecuting Labor Trafficking Cases

The above cases of immigration and visa violations highlight not only the profile of potential labor trafficking cases, but the downside to prosecuting these potential labor trafficking cases as visa or immigration offenses. To begin, the potential labor trafficking cases that are being identified in St. Louis and the surrounding communities are generally associated with industrial labor. In particular, the industrial labor that has been identified has been charged in conjunction with visas based on employment contracts that ultimately turn into forced servitude, fraud businesses, or scams trying to prove that they need to legitimately bring people into the United States. Although social service providers insinuated that involuntary domestic servitude is occurring in St. Louis and the metro east, it is not commonly prosecuted as such. Social service providers have acknowledged this gap and are working to identify the cross-connection between sex trafficking and labor trafficking, but as of this writing, the majority of cases being prosecuted in St. Louis and the surrounding communities are sex trafficking cases despite the potential for an underlying labor trafficking offense.

In addition to the types of potential labor trafficking cases identified in St. Louis those who are actually investigating the cases are of central importance. As already discussed earlier in the chapter, when victims of labor trafficking reach their destination, whether it is through migration patterns or fraudulent promises of work, their enslavement is localized. Given this, "the identification of labor trafficking victims normally is more effectively handled by local law enforcement officers during routine inspections and investigations, as well as through local tips and surveillance of local businesses" (Polaris Project, 2013). Unfortunately, cases in St. Louis and the surrounding communities are not being investigated by local level law enforcement. Rather, they are being investigated as federal immigration and/or visa violations. Of the local law enforcement officials interviewed for this project, not a single officer contended to investigating labor trafficking cases. Most law enforcement officials stated that they were sure that labor trafficking was occurring in St. Louis and or the metro-east, but believed that it was not a priority. According to one officer, "the labor part is, I mean I know it's out there, but I've never encountered it in 20 years, you know with major case, we've never run across anything with that" (see Chapter Four for a detailed discussion of law enforcement and labor trafficking). However, as one advocate stated so precisely, "just because [labor trafficking cases] haven't come across your desk doesn't mean it's not happening in your county." Advocates were encountering labor trafficking, yet officers were not, as they were not actively working to identify or investigate it.

Lastly, there is a fundamental issue regarding the sentencing patterns related to visa and immigration violations versus the federal sentencing guidelines for labor trafficking. According to 18 U.S. Code § 1589, anyone who "knowingly provides or obtains the labor or services of a person" by force fraud or coercion, "shall be fined under this title, imprisoned not more than 20 years, or both. If death results from a violation of this section, or if the violation includes kidnaping, an attempt to kidnap, aggravated sexual abuse, or an attempt to kill, the defendant shall be fined under this title, imprisoned for any term of years or life, or both" (18 U.S. Code § 1589). Cases that have been prosecuted in Missouri as visa or immigration offense carry a sentence ranging from misdemeanor penalties to fines and restitution. Only in *United States of America v. Abrorkhodja Askarkhodjaev* (2011) in which the RICO Act was used was there a penalty that closely matched the federal sentencing guidelines for labor trafficking.

Aside from the general issues of how labor trafficking cases are perceived in St. Louis and the surrounding communities, social service providers and law enforcement officials alike have identified general problems associated with handling labor trafficking in the community. As stated earlier, the main problem is identifying the victims. As one social service provider explained, "[it is] just getting into those insular ethnic communities [that] has been difficult … in this area, especially where the communities are really tight knit. And it's hard for outsiders or U.S. workers to try and help an outreach. It's been difficult." Part of the problem with connecting with the various communities is that some community members are afraid to speak out against the victimization. According to a legal advocate, "I think neighbors think it's none of their business, you know. Or maybe the neighbors are doing it themselves, or they have relatives that have trafficked relatives." A social service provider expressed a similar sentiment claiming that "one of the challenges of reaching into the ethnic communities is usually the traffickers are of the same ethnicity, and so it is a little dicey." Lastly, the labor trafficking victim may not come forward to authorities because he/she does not believe that he/she has been trafficked. These key issues have contributed to the hidden nature of human trafficking and the lack of identification in St. Louis and the surrounding communities.

Outreach Efforts

Despite the problems associated with identifying labor trafficking cases, social service providers and legal advocates have taken measures to educate potential victims of labor trafficking. Most of the outreach efforts that have been identified took place in the rural sector, although closer to St. Louis, efforts are being made to educate first responders on indicators of labor trafficking. In the rural communities, social service providers take every effort to educate not only citizens who are likely to come into contact with labor trafficking victims, but also the potential victims themselves. As one social service provider stated, "I go to trucking schools to do presentations. I go to beauty schools, to migrant camps, you name it!" Anyone who is willing to listen can be trained.

One of the main locations to present outreach has been the hotels where the migrant laborers may be living. Therefore, social service providers attempt to create strong relationships with the hotel owners and managers.

> 84 West motel here houses a large number of migrant workers. We got [the manager] on board ... [T]hey have bar-b-q grills and hammocks, and they cook out, so he's given access [to us] to go over in the evenings and afternoons anytime we want ... We go there, we have hygiene kits, and we're distributing those as the connection with the farmworker population.

Other advocates not only go to housing, but also to the places of employment:

> We usually go out to the orchards or to their housing. A lot of the housing is at the orchard, but not in the orchard. They live nearby but don't all work for the same employer. They go to different farms. So, we go when they are leaving the work at the end of the day and start passing out calendars, let them know who we are, how to contact us, and how we can help. Sometimes we go during lunch,

but their lunch break is short—at most an hour. And we don't want to disturb them.

In general, the response from the farmers to the advocates speaking with the migrant workers varies.

There have been some issues of employers asking you to leave. This wasn't me, but I know of one case where the employer got on a truck and almost ran over one of our workers. Sometimes they will be hostile, but other times, they are fine. They will come up to us and ask us who we are, what are we doing ... We tell them what we are doing, and they are like OK.

Other crew leaders that have been identified as having poor labor practices create a blacklist of social service providers so that they cannot come and speak with the migrant workers. As one social service provider recollected:

I was banned from the camp eventually ... Department of Labor ended up coming [into the camp] at some point. I guess someone must have reported them ... but it wasn't me that day! They took about 14 people out of the field and they were going to question them ... [T]he farmer thought it was me, and banned me from the camp. And he said [to me], '... I know it was you, and I know you're the one that probably called in the department of labor.' And I said, 'no, really, I didn't.' And he said, 'well, you are not allowed back in the camp!' So anybody that went in ... any agency ... I would tell them, 'he will ask you if you know me and you're gonna think he's being friendly, but if you say yes, he'll say you're not coming in!' And that's what he did.

Getting the farmers on board with outreach has probably been the most difficult for advocates in the rural communities. According to an advocate:

Getting these farmers is like pulling teeth ... It's just hard to get the farmers involved ... I don't think they're gonna

take time unless they think they are gonna be held responsible for some kind of labor issue that's being pulled off
by their contractor or crew leader ... They talk to the contractor, the guy calls, 'when you coming in, I need this
many people,' and that's it. I don't think they really know
and it's kind of rude to say, but I don't know if they really
care. I mean they want the workers in, they want them
out, they don't want any conflict or turmoil. 'Get my
crop,' you know. 'I'll pay you so I can get paid.'

Although there have been efforts to get the farmers involved in the
training, at the time of this writing, it has still proven to be a difficult, if not impossible task.

In St. Louis and the surrounding communities, outreach is limited with regards to labor trafficking. However, coalition groups
are now working with law enforcement and providing trainings on
indicators of a potential labor trafficking case. Some other agencies
are working on the education aspect with the foreign born population, but overall, the outreach efforts have been extremely limited
in St. Louis and the surrounding communities. (To read more
about outreach efforts and training, see Chapter Five.)

Chapter Summary

Labor trafficking is under-identified, mislabeled, and well hidden in St. Louis and the bi-state area. In the rural communities,
labor trafficking has been identified in the orchards, chicken factories, and restaurants. Crew leaders and managers trap migrant
workers with tactics such as holding of wages and personal documents. Unfortunately, because of the mobility of the migrant population, witnesses and potential victims are routinely lost.

Close to St. Louis and the surrounding communities, labor trafficking is less likely to be investigated in comparison to sex trafficking. Even in those cases where there may be an overlap between
sex trafficking and labor trafficking, generally, only the sex trafficking aspect will be investigated and prosecuted. Labor violations
in the industrial sector that have been identified are investigated

and prosecuted as visa and labor violations, which provide minimal sentencing and a weak deterrent for the perpetrator.

Outreach efforts are being made in the rural communities, but advocates and social service providers have hit a wall when trying to work with the farmers. In St. Louis and the surrounding communities, the trend is shifting to start focusing on training on indicators of labor trafficking victimization, but at the time of this writing, much work still needs to be done with regards to outreach efforts in the city and surrounding communities. Such efforts are being made to make contact in the isolated communities, as well as educate those who are most likely to have first contact with potential victims.

Overall, labor trafficking is occurring in St. Louis and the bistate area. Every individual interviewed for this project stated that they were sure it was happening beneath the surface, but it is extremely difficult to identify. Once identified, it is even more difficult to maintain contact with victims and witnesses. Given the isolated and hidden nature of labor trafficking, the best that can be done is to continue to educate the public, law enforcement, social service providers, and others likely to come into contact with labor trafficked people on the indicators and begin to look at human trafficking in conjunction with sex trafficking. The victims of labor trafficking are very real, and need to be identified and protected from those who prey and capitalize on their vulnerable status.

Chapter 3

Sex Trafficking

"So, I was like, pretty much kicked out of my house at like, fourteen. I mean, technically, I left, but, like, they wanted to send me back to gay camp, where they try to 'get the gay out of you.' Like, I knew that wasn't possible, and I was like, I just don't belong here. I tried to go to Chicago, hitched [hitchhiking], and ended up in a homeless shelter, and the situation up there just wasn't good, so I came back to Missouri, this time to St. Louis. And there are men, I can tell you, much older men who are looking for kids just like [I was], who don't know what to do or where to go, living in doorways, abandoned houses, homeless shelters, hotel lobbies, even people's cars if the doors are unlocked, and they offer you things. Like a meal, or, 'Hey come back to my place for a while, you can stay with me,' but it's not for nothing. They want sex for it. And I did that, because I had nothing else. I had nothing. I got picked up outside a homeless shelter, and in a doorway, just sitting outside. That was it, like, was my introduction to like sex and also sex work. And I thought he loved me, because he protected me, gave me things, was nice to me, but then, looking back, he was out looking for me, I could have been anyone."

—Gay-Identified Male Survivor

Through analysis of narratives like this, Chapter Three examines sex trafficking in the St. Louis bi-state area, including the backgrounds of survivors, types of sex trafficking identified, risk factors, and techniques of traffickers. Sex trafficking survivors come from an array of different backgrounds, and include girls, boys, and adults of varying races, classes, cultures, sexual orientations and gender identities. Individuals are sex-trafficked in a variety of regions, including rural, suburban, and urban areas of the St. Louis bi-state area. Like many regions across the midwestern United States, sex trafficking in St. Louis and the surrounding communities most commonly involves women and youth who are United States citizens. The types of sex trafficking in St. Louis and the surrounding communities take different forms, such as pimp-controlled prostitution, survival sex, and pornography. Trafficking is perpetrated by boyfriends, parents, pimps, and buyers. Chapter Three also provides a sociological analysis of sex trafficking in the region, including the ways weak social institutions work to produce social environments conducive to sex trafficking vulnerability. Such risk factors include weak education, economic, and family systems combined with a lack of social safety nets, which work in tandem to increase the risk of sex trafficking vulnerability. Traffickers target vulnerabilities, such as poverty, runaway or throwaway status, disability, and homelessness. They use emotional and physical abuses to both recruit victims and provide barriers to leaving. Further, traffickers use the Internet and interstate movement to control and conduct trafficking operations, and particularly to avoid detection. Drawing from prosecuted cases of sex trafficking and interviews with 31 anti-trafficking professionals and survivors in the St. Louis region, this chapter examines sex trafficking in St. Louis and the surrounding bi-state area. The chapter begins by describing the survivors of sex trafficking victimization.

Who Are the Survivors?

The St. Louis bi-state area includes the urban city environment of St. Louis, surrounded by wealthy, middle, and working class suburbs, spreading out to small river towns, rural farming districts, and trailer parks. From the areas of the city with dilapidated buildings, wrought with neglect and crime, to small river and farming towns and suburban neighborhoods—the picture of the heartland—sex trafficking was found to occur everywhere. One of the most common themes uncovered in interviewing various professionals across the social service and justice system sectors was that sex trafficking in St. Louis encompassed a broad array of victim demographics that spanned race, class, region, sex, sexual orientation, and gender identity.

While people from a variety of different backgrounds experienced sex trafficking, the majority of respondents indicated that cases disproportionately involved domestically trafficked women and girls. Different organizations seemed to work with different demographic groups, possibly due to the area of the St. Louis bi-state region that they worked in, the nature of their organization, or how their clients came into contact with them. For example, the executive director of The Covering House, an organization providing services for trafficked/commercially sexually exploited girls stated:

There's a lot more to it [sex trafficking] than people realize, and people want to sometimes sit in judgment thinking, 'not my daughter,' or, 'it's not going to happen here.' We've learned quickly that the demographic isn't always what people typically think too, like you know, inner city children who maybe are from impoverished neighborhoods. Certainly they are, [but] most of our clients have come from the County [St. Louis County] and/or small towns.

This organization, located in the City of St. Louis, predominately served girls in suburban St. Louis county or small towns throughout neighboring counties, belying the popular image of the Midwest and small town America. The majority of girls who came to The Covering House were brought by their parents, although cases also came through referrals from other community organizations. Yet, another respondent working in a social service oriented organization in St. Louis City indicated that the majority of his clients were homeless males and females, who were largely inner city African American teens. Two individuals working in the family courts in St. Louis city indicated they typically worked with inner-city African American girls in the sex trafficking cases they encountered, which is expected as it is a city court, and the city population is predominately African American (U.S. Census Bureau, 2014). Overall, sex trafficking survivors were found in differing regions and among all demographic groups. Prosecuted cases involving sex trafficking or related charges in the St. Louis bi-state area support this claim as well, involving individuals from various social backgrounds and regions, including urban, rural, suburban, or small-town environments. However, while anyone is potentially at risk, risk factors are higher for some groups compared to others. It cannot be ignored that a disproportionate number of victims in the St. Louis area were female African American youth, at least as depicted in federally prosecuted cases. This finding coincides with multiple research studies conducted in Chicago, Minneapolis, Los Angeles, St. Louis, and Hartford (Oselin, 2014; Raphael, 2008, 2010; Hughes, 2005; Martin & Pierce, 2014). This is consistent with national federal data, finding that while African Americans make up roughly thirteen percent of the population, they compose forty percent of sex trafficking victims (U.S. Department of Justice, 2013).

Illustrating survivor characteristics in further depth, a social service provider, the director of operations at The Covering House, indicated that clients held multiple identities and backgrounds. She further emphasized that sex trafficking not only involved people of various identities, but also took multiple forms that differed from the popular discourse:

> I think we're seeing all different types of victimologies. I walked in trying to have a very broad view and realized that even my view was too narrow ... we've had clients from every socio-economic background, several different races, several different cultures and experiences ... everything from a girl who is a runaway to a girl that is in high school and an athlete and actively involved. So it comes in a lot of different forms, and I think that's the thing with exploitation is it, trafficking, we sometimes have a very narrow view, but that word exploitation, I think kind of creates more of a gray area, and we see a lot more of a variety of how it's happening. It's not always just ... I think we often think of it as being a girl that's held against her will, and it's not always in a physical way. A lot of times our girls are held against their will in a more emotional/psychological way than physically.

In fact, many interviewees noted that the popular conception of sex trafficking was not what they typically saw in their work with survivors, and noted that a broader context for defining and understanding sex trafficking was important to understand and address the problem. The public discourse and awareness campaigns often depict images of girls in chains, symbolic of the coercion involved in sex trafficking (Doezema, 2005; Hoyle et al, 2011; Nichols, 2015). For example, the director of The Covering House, which provides services for commercially sexually exploited girls under the age of eighteen, stated:

> There's ... and I think probably the other question is: Do you think that the definition of trafficking is accurate, and my answer to that would have been it's much broader than what the average person thinks. They think it's like the Liam Neeson rescue of Taken and have someone grabbed off of the streets. And we've seen so much here, it's so much more through the coercion and manipulation.

She explained that she did encounter people who were physically held captive by their traffickers, but the spectrum was much broader, particularly involving psychological manipulation and control, similar to the psychological abuses and coercive control involved in situations of intimate partner violence (see Raphael & Myers-Powell, 2010; Lloyd, 2012; Martin & Pierce, 2014). Another social service provider who worked with commercially sexually exploited youth also indicated that the popular discourse did not depict the multifaceted, or even typical, cases of sex trafficking:

> Yeah ... yeah ... so, you know, considering that Federal definition that any minor involved in the commercial sex act can be considered a trafficking victim, we see actually quite a bit of it, you know, it doesn't look like your typical, like media pieces where maybe they're kidnapped, or maybe they're forced into this, that there is a gun to their head, or something like that, although we do see that too.

Another social service provider maintained:

> I saw a movie one time or I don't even think I watched it, but a preview for it, about and it was a white female who had been sort of kidnapped and her father was out looking for her, and I was just like, you know that is something that I'm sure it happens, but it's sooo not what I experience or see here ...

This social service provider described his typical client as a minor involved in a form of trafficking commonly described as survival sex, in which someone sells sex or is exploited by others out of a need for shelter, food, or clothing. Yet another social service provider gave a similar response:

> My personal experience has not been ... I think oftentimes when people talk about sex trafficking they think about someone being like kidnapped and forced to do something and held in like complete ... locks and chains and all of that. And that has not been what I.... that's not my population, I'm sure that probably exists....

When asked why the popular depictions of sex trafficking, in both the media and in awareness campaigns, depicted sex trafficking in a narrow way, one social service provider stated:

> You know I mean I think different things speak differently to different people. So, if the chains analogy really grabs the attention of someone that maybe wouldn't have otherwise known about human trafficking, then okay. But I do think it confuses the matter and doesn't depict clearly who the actual victims are, and it draws attention away from the conversation we really need to be having around the overlap between trafficking and prostitution and where they are the same and where they are different. And I think that, you know, it really also distances us from what it really looks like because I think it makes you think of something happening in maybe a developing country, or in someone's basement in a neighborhood that you

know nothing about. Whereas, really, like it maybe is the person you just passed on the street. It may be happening in your neighborhood. It may be way closer to home. And I definitely think that I wouldn't go so far as to say that it is negatively impacting our movement, but I do think it can draw attention away from and distract from the real conversation. And it's very feelings-based … it grabs people's attention, it makes them feel something, which isn't necessarily negative either … And I think just a lot of money and conversation is misdirected.

According to the respondents in this study, cases involving confinement or physical restraint only represent a fraction of sex trafficking cases. Social service providers who worked with survivors noted that these cases were either rare, or they didn't see them at all.

While these cases were uncommon, it is important to note that they did occur. A social service provider noted that a survivor she worked with was held captive in a gated residence with alarms and guards:

> … I mean, she wasn't allowed to leave. She wasn't allowed to, you know, make phone calls or have access. She was held up in a place, but it had alarms—it had high fences with alarms …

A survivor, who was also a social service provider, indicated she experienced confinement as well:

> And even though I am a survivor of that myself, you know, my experience was so brief that I wasn't really indoctrinated into a culture, it was more like, 'Just let me out of this room!'

In addition, one federally prosecuted case involved a disabled woman confined and held in a closet in the St. Louis area by the brother-and-sister trafficking team of now-convicted traffickers Carla and Carl Mathews (U.S. Attorney's Office, Eastern District of Missouri, 2014). While cases of confinement represent a smaller proportion of cases, the experiences of survivors who have experienced this form of trafficking should not be minimized. Rather, it is important to conceptualize sex trafficking holistically, representing this type of trafficking as one of the multiple forms sex trafficking can take to avoid mischaracterization of the issue. Participants described typical cases as involving teen girls who were romanced by older men and then channeled into prostitution, or girls, boys, and adults in economically vulnerable positions engaging in survival sex. These typical cases of sex trafficking, as well as other types of sex trafficking, are described in detail in the following section.

Types of Sex Trafficking

According to the U.S. Trafficking Victims Protection Act (TVPA), sex trafficking is primarily defined as any commercial sex act involving a minor, or an adult who engages in a commercial sex act as a result of force, fraud, or coercion. Sex trafficking in the St. Louis bi-state region involved commercial sex in the forms of prostitution and pornography. Traffickers included pimps, boyfriends, parents, and buyers. Pimp-controlled prostitution, the "boyfriend pimp," survival sex, parents-as-traffickers, false-front fraud schemes, and pornography were implicated as types of sex trafficking found throughout the area. This typology of sex trafficking is detailed in the subsections below.

Pimp-Controlled Prostitution and the "Boyfriend" Pimp

The majority of social service providers who worked with sex trafficking survivors maintained that pimps posing as boyfriends represented one of the most common forms of sex trafficking they encountered. In such cases, men presented themselves first as a romantic partner, taking girls and women on dates, buying them nice things, and treating them as a girlfriend. In time, this intimate relationship would develop into a sex trafficking situation. Boyfriends then acted as pimps, finding dates for and facilitating prostitution of both minors and adults. Many of these cases involved older men as "boyfriends" who pimped teenage girls. Other cases involved similarly aged intimate partners, and the boyfriend forced or coerced the prostitution, essentially pimping his girl-friend. Both of these scenarios could be viewed as extensions of intimate partner violence, encompassing emotional, sexual, eco-nomic, and physical abuse. When asked what a typical case looked like, the Director of the Juvenile Division of the Family Courts maintained:

> Typically it's an older male that probably has led the girls to believe that they are special and that they buy them things. They do their hair, they get their nails done, they have them dancing on the East side. Those things that teenage girls like.

Romancing the girls, making them feel desirable and cared for, was a technique pimps used to win the affections of the girls. An-other social service provider, the executive director of The Cover-ing House, which provides services to trafficked or exploited girls, also indicated the most common scenario involved older men be-friending young teen girls. However, she additionally noted cases which involved boys their own age as well, who got them involved in prostitution:

> Mmm hmmm. Or an older friend where we actually have had to say listen, he's 52 and you're 13, he's not your friend. But to them they love them. In their mind they really do love them and they really do trust them, and so, we've seen more of those cases. We've actually had more of like stereotypical type of cases where they've been lured in and taken off. And we're seeing a lot of those cases come through where the boyfriend that is the one ... and sometimes the boyfriend is not an older guy, a lot of times it is, but sometimes it's the guy that is sit-ting next to her in class ... Yeah a lot of times, especially recently, we're seeing a lot of cases where it's the boyfriend and ... it's the, 'I love you, I'm your boyfriend,' just like any high school girl would think of

it, and then, it goes into, 'Here's a way that you could help,' or 'We could go to a nice dinner if you did this.' And we're seeing it ... where girls, that their boyfriends are using them to pay off debts on the street, or their boyfriend is selling them out of the backseat of a car. Sometimes it's that graphic and sometimes he will literally send them to the front door of the house. And nobody is none the wiser, like they don't know that it's happening because it's ... the boy sitting next to her in regular school. So I think it's kind of all over the spectrum. And sometimes it's, 'I'm going to lure you away from your parents,' and sometimes it looks like a normal girlfriend/boyfriend relationship.

Similar to this illustration, social service providers, justice system officials, and survivors consistently indicated one of the most common types of sex trafficking cases in the St. Louis area involved pimp control, usually with the pimp doubling as a boyfriend or friend. This finding is not unique, as a growing body of work examining domestic sex trafficking also finds this pattern (Martin & Pierce, 2014; Raphael & Myers Powell, 2010; Lloyd, 2012; Kotrla, 2010; Raphael, 2008; Smith et al, 2009; Oselin, 2014).

A social service provider who worked primarily with older teens and young adults also described the pimp-as-boyfriend as what a typical case of sex trafficking looked like, but elaborated by highlighting foster care, homelessness, and runaway status as risk factors for this form of sex trafficking:

Typically what I see are 17-year-olds and older, so qualified minors up to adults who experienced abuse and neglect as children, or are in and out of foster care, and then, once they became somewhere in that cycle, someone entered and whether that was when they were in foster care as a child, or now that they are out on the streets ... as kind of that partner, i.e., boyfriend figure, who also encourages and assists with the exploitation, basically. So,

whether that's pimping them out or finding them johns,
I would say that's probably what I see the most.

Adult women who experienced trafficking were found to have
been typically trafficked first in their youth, also by the "boyfriend"
pimp. A social service provider who worked with women leaving
prostitution noted when asked what she saw with the adult population of trafficking survivors:

> ... I've been trying to work with a young woman who
> lives in adjoining county who was first raped by her uncle
> at the age of 13, entered into prostitution shortly there-
> after at the urging of a boyfriend, and he then controlled
> her for about 11 years, mostly in Las Vegas and New Jersey
> and California. He also fathered her two children ...

The same social service provider elaborated on her experiences
working with clients who were adult women, stating that the
"boyfriend" experience was the most typical form of sex trafficking
she encountered in her work with survivors:

> It's really common, at least in my experience, and my in-
> terviews with people and just talking with women, it's
> very common that's how it starts out. You know it's the
> older boyfriend, I'm in love, let's move here, and then,
> you know wining and dining after a couple of months,
> and drugs are typically involved at this point, and then it's
> like, here's what you're going to have to do to earn your
> keep. And then, a lot of the women will still call them
> their boyfriends, but in actuality they're pimps, but it's
> sometimes difficult for the girls or the women to make
> that distinction, because they won't identify, you know,
> they won't identify as being pimp-controlled. Or as vic-
> tims or survivors for that matter, sometimes not until
> years later.

In sum, the boyfriend-as-pimp scenario was described as a
common form of sex trafficking in the St. Louis area, and could
be viewed as an extension of intimate partner violence among mi-

nors and adults (see Nichols & Heil, 2014; Raphael, 2010). Multiple prosecuted cases of sex trafficking, described throughout this chapter, involved pimp-control without an intimate relationship (U.S. Attorney's Office, Eastern District of Missouri, 2014). Like the "pimp-as-boyfriend," this dynamic also overlapped with survival sex. Survival sex was also described as one of the most common forms of sex trafficking in the St. Louis bi-state area as well, which sometimes overlapped with the pimp-as-boyfriend form of sex trafficking or pimp-controlled prostitution that did not involve a boyfriend.

Survival Sex

Survival sex is the term used to describe trading sex for something of value related to basic needs, such as food, shelter, money, or clothing. The choice to engage in sex work can at times be a socially conditioned choice. Runaways are those who voluntarily leave home, and throwaways are those whose parents ask or force them to leave home (Kotrla, 2010; Nichols, 2015; Smith et al, 2009). Runaways and throwaways are particularly exploitable for a number of reasons. First, throwaways are unlikely to be looked for or reported as missing, as their parents asked them to leave in the first place. Further, it is difficult for minors under the age of sixteen to find legitimate employment due to child labor laws. Typically, working under the age of sixteen requires a note from school and consent of a parent or guardian. Importantly, runaway teens don't want to be found or sent back home, and will not get the consent of a parent or guardian, so legitimate employment is largely blocked for minors under sixteen. Minors who run away from home, particularly those who are involved in prostitution, often do so because of abuse, conflict, rejection, or neglect in the home (Smith et al., 2008; Kotrla, 2010; Nichols, 2015). Consequently, in order to avoid returning to conflict-ridden homes, minors find ways to survive in the streets or by staying randomly with friends and strangers—what is commonly called "couch surfing." In order to get basic necessities, such youth or adults who have nothing else at times sell sex. This finding is consistent with prior work, also finding survival sex as a prevalent form of sex trafficking or prostitution (Curtis, 2008; Oselin, 2014; Marcus et al, 2014; Raphael & Myers Powell, 2010; Smith, Vardaman, & Snow, 2009). According to survivors, pimps and buyers in the St. Louis area appear to be actively searching for runaway or truant youth, or those who appear to be in need of basic necessities. A social service provider at The Covering House maintained that survival sex was common in the cases they worked with:

> ... a lot of the girls that we're seeing most recently are high run risk and are runaways. And so a lot of it has been finding shelter, and usually it's a guy that says, 'Well, I have a way that I can give you shelter ...'

In this illustration, typical of respondents, pimps or buyers would find those in need of money, shelter, and basic survival necessities. Pimps would pose as a romantic caretaker figure or a friend, and would introduce them shortly thereafter into prostitution. Buyers would offer money, a place to stay, or food in exchange for sex. Exploitation of vulnerabilities was highlighted repeatedly throughout the interviews.

Social service providers and those working in the justice system indicated that women and girls engaged in survival sex, but young men and teen boys experienced sex trafficking in the form of survival sex as well. In such cases, the males were usually gay-identified, and had older male clients, although women were also found to exploit straight-identified males, and straight-identified males sometimes had older male clients, engaging in what is informally known as "gay for pay." One social service provider, who largely worked with homeless or at risk youth, described a typical case involving a male:

> So they identify typically in a very different way, and I found them, at least, and this is all anecdotally and just from my caseload, but much less apt to talk about it or but ... just if not more traumatized by it, because I think there are so many standards of what masculinity is and this is something that they will ask why, why did this happen to me or why couldn't I have fought back, or why I

couldn't.... lots of internalized guilt, loss, oppression, trauma, pain ... you name it ... but yes definitely, because so many of these kids are in situations where they are just trying to survive and highly vulnerable and taken advantage of and exploited. So, it really does not matter what their sex is.

While in some cases males had pimps, several social service providers noted that overall male victims were much less likely, or even unlikely, to have pimps, and indicated it was usually an older adult who exploited them sexually in exchange for a place to stay and food to eat. Consistently, survival sex was reported as the most common form of sex trafficking experienced by boys. Another social service provider delineated:

I don't know if there are pimps in those cases, that does not mean that they're not there, but no, it's typically adult men and women who are basically forcing them to have sex with them to have maybe a safe place, or food or a candy bar or something like that, just so that they can eat or get off the street. Women and men that ... engage in that, for sure with the males.

Further, LGBTQ youth may be particularly vulnerable to survival sex, with an increased likelihood of runaway or throwaway status related to non-acceptance of their sexual orientation or gender identity in their homes (NCTSN, 2006; NRCPFC, 2012). Another survivor recounted his experiences as a young same-sex oriented teen, coming from a problematic home life. His parents and his school did not accept his same-sex sexual orientation, and he was homeless as a teen as a result of his mistreatment. He recalled being sexually exploited by older men out of a need for both emotional attachments and a need to survive:

I was homeless also as a teenager, it was more like a personal experience navigating sort of the systems that are here in place, and I think in that way I definitely can share that.... so when I think of sex trafficking you think of like

youth being sort of pulled into, like, very Law & Order
SVU, like they're hidden and like, they're hidden in some
basement and they're tied in chains or they're thrown into
a truck, right. I don't know of any experiences like that.
Now, when we think of like … sex work or like more of
getting that young person their autonomy maybe in a
sense, it definitely is going on. In fact, I know that's going
on, and where I think that's prevalent, and specifically as
a gay man, I think that it happens a lot with men who
prey on younger queer, gay men and boys. So that young
people are sleeping with much older men. I think it's
more for love, right. So, like, part of it sometimes is to
feel loved. It's to, like, have a mentor figure. I think sometimes it's definitely for survival.

This example illustrates vulnerability may be heightened for
LGBTQ youth, who may be rejected by their parents and run away
or are asked to leave their homes. This homelessness may produce
a social environment conducive to survival sex, or exploitation by
buyers. Pointedly, like girls who get involved with a pimp-as-
boyfriend looking for love, affection, or to meet some emotional
need, male gay-identified and transgender youth may also be
drawn to an older man offering affection and mentorship, as well
as food and shelter. The same respondent elaborated on his experiences, noting buyers who actively sought out vulnerable homeless
gay and transgender youth, for commercial sex:

I mean Coffee Cartel, not so much anymore, but when I
was coming out like 12 or 13 years ago, the Coffee Cartel
was the only LGBTQ coffee house, and then, there was
something really kind of beautiful about like, in the summer, people would like drive in from St. Charles County
and West County and all of the counties to drive past Coffee Cartel because if you were sitting outside Coffee Cartel
at night you are out as being queer, right. So now it's not
that way. I mean there are yuppies and straight people and
college people, so much gentrification has happened so a
place like that now doesn't exist there. I know like 12 or

13 years ago, because it is a 24-hour coffee shop, it sort of acts like a Dunkin Donuts does in urban cities. Where like these kids who really don't have no place to stay will go and hang out there; or they don't necessarily have a bed to sleep in but they need to like cool off for a while, they need the access or the ability to use a restroom to clean themselves. So they will go pop in those private restrooms that they have ... they are really strategic and smart that they have those, you know what I mean, youth know like where can I go to keep myself safe? Libraries are another place too. So, I think like those situations I definitely seen like, scheming looking men, honestly I say men, because I can't think of a situation where I personally saw or experienced what I perceive a woman or someone who is female doing this. So it's like men who I think do what I call trolling the coffee shops or trolling those areas kind of looking for these youth who are vulnerable offering them money for whatever, oftentimes the youth will do it. I know from myself, that was something that happened to me when I was a young person. So, that's kind of more, I think, the niche of St. Louis and from what I see.

Buyers were described as purposefully searching spots where homeless LGBTQ youth were likely to frequent, either to access a safe space open 24 hours, or a space to use the bathroom and clean up. The aim of the buyer was to take advantage of this vulnerable position and engage the youth in survival sex. When something of value is traded for sex, and involves minors, this legally constitutes sex trafficking. The irony illustrated in this quote is that a landmark that was known as beautiful as a space for openly expressing gay identities, and as a safe space for LGBTQ homeless youth to go, was simultaneously exploited by buyers for the same reasons.

Shades of Gray

In cases involving adults, survival sex was viewed by some research participants as a hazy area. With those under 18, this "survival sex" is legally considered sex trafficking, although it was also referred to as commercial sexual exploitation of children (CSEC) within the advocacy and social services communities in the St. Louis area. With adults, survival sex was more likely to be described as "exploitation" or "sex work" as opposed to sex trafficking, as there was some level of consent, albeit socially conditioned consent based upon economic need. Respondents in this study struggled with the compartmentalization of "sex trafficking," "sexual exploitation," and "sex work." Many social service providers described these characterizations, and the difficulty in labeling them, as "shades of gray." There is an abundance of polarized, highly ideologically charged academic work exploring these intricacies (Madden-Dempsey, 2011; Weitzer, 2010; Ekberg, 2004; Outshoorn, 2010; Oselin, 2014; Marcus et al, 2014).

Respondents in this study generally recognized that survival sex among adults was willful and there was consent (legally minors cannot consent). Yet respondents also recognized some level of exploitation, in that buyers would offer assistance, but only in exchange for sex. Moreover, buyers and pimps were actively looking for vulnerable people who would be willing to engage in sex-for-survival. This was viewed as taking advantage of an economically marginalized person. In fact, many respondents noted the importance of recognizing the subtle distinctions between sex trafficking and sexual exploitation, noting that those engaging in survival sex were doing so out of economic necessity. The line between exploitation and sex work, some respondents noted, was based upon the perceptions of the people they worked with. One social service provider noted:

> And it gets really hazy. I think then if we're talking about adults versus minors and things like that; because if it's an adult it kind of depends to me on how they are defining their situation ... to me as a social worker the client's view is the one that I am going to take on and perceive it to be.

For some social service providers, if an individual viewed themselves as a sex worker, regardless of economic need, they would accept that view, with the exception of minors, where survival sex was generally seen as a form of sex trafficking. If an adult they were working with clearly had few choices, and selling sex made them unhappy, respondents typically viewed this as exploitation.

> And my experience is just more with like people who like I can think of a lot of people who maybe they're 18, they don't have a family or not a family that's not a very positive influence, not supportive, doesn't want them, disowns them, whatever the case is ... who they might get involved in this and there is some element of choice along the way, but it's also choices that are made in the context of not having a lot of choices ... for people who are homeless or for people who are just even economically [struggling] ...

Similarly, a survivor pointed out, "And when you don't have opportunities and you are in a situation where society doesn't allow for further opportunities then that's what you're going to do to survive. Out of desperation." Another social service provider also indicated that at times it was difficult to compartmentalize his client's experiences, and to distinguish between sex work and exploitive prostitution based on few choices:

> So I also worked with another young gay man, grew up in a rural community, conservative Christian family, kicked out and then I think he ended up like, his family wouldn't even register him for high school. So he had to wait until he was 18 and then register himself for high school. Like the kid just did so many amazing things, in terms of like literally pulling himself up by his bootstraps. So anyway, very similar story [to a previous story in the interview] where he was just really financially struggling and had been doing so just kind of spinning for years and not really able to get himself out of, into a stable living situation and everything, and so, for him, he was mostly doing like erotic massage and sometimes he was having sex, but it was definitely not with one person like with the previous

person I was talking about, but was with a lot of different people and ... he was basically working as a sex worker ...

Stories involving "shades of gray" with adults who engaged in sex work because of poverty permeated the experiences of the social service providers who worked with them. Poverty was seen as a driving factor for prostitution, with some exceptions. For example, a few social service providers noted that some sex workers enjoyed their occupations, outside of fulfilling an economic need, particularly transgender sex workers:

> I think it is hard to sometimes tease out where does commercial exploitation or sex trafficking start, and where does sex work ... how is that different? And I think that I've worked with some clients who identify as sex workers or ... I also work with a lot of transgender clients, who might identify as 'call girls' or as they all have different words for it, but ... so some people are on that end of the spectrum like it is almost something that they view as almost their career, that they really like it ...

Yet, respondents consistently indicated that many others did not, and acknowledged some level of exploitation, as their clients were engaging in sex work solely out of economic need. One social service provider illustrated:

> I think St. Louis has a really large homeless youth population. Young people that do identify as LGBTQ, a lot of the youth ... have indicated at some point or other that they have been homeless or that they're at sort of the threat of being homeless or being kicked out of their house for their sexual orientation or gender identity. And so, definitely I would say it's something that is kind of covert ... But definitely I think for young people who are disenfranchised and feeling disempowered and don't have a lot of resources at their availability, like.... I use the word 'sex work' so sex work I think is something that is either placed on them, or something they may choose, depending on sort of what options they feel that they have.

Accordingly, whether or not other options were available, or if the individual was a minor, or how the client labeled their own situation determined some social service providers' views on if an individual was sex trafficked, sexually exploited, or a sex worker.

Many social service providers in this study indicated that providing services to exploited individuals was just as important as providing services to those who more clearly fit the legal terms of sex trafficking. In fact, when the Rescue and Restore Coalition split, largely due to shifting grant requirements, the newly formed organization was named the Coalition Against Trafficking and Exploitation in part as a public commitment to educating others about the importance of recognizing and assisting sexually exploited people.

Buyers as Sex Traffickers

In cases of survival sex, a buyer may be implicated in sex trafficking. In fact, buyers have been charged with sex trafficking in the St. Louis bi-state area. For example, in one case Patrick Sekula, a fifty-five-year-old man from rural Imperial, Missouri, texted an undercover officer who Sekula thought was a fifteen-year-old girl, and attempted to convince the "girl" to have sex with him for $60. He was charged in St. Louis County with the attempted sex trafficking of a child in this sting operation. Similarly, in St. Charles County, a largely suburban area neighboring St. Louis, has also prosecuted buyers as sex traffickers. Twenty-three-year-old Mohammad Teimoortagh was charged with the sex trafficking of a child under the age of eighteen when he attempted to arrange a sexual encounter with a minor. He faced additional related charges, including first degree promoting prostitution and statutory rape. The Illinois side of the bi-state area has prosecuted buyers as sex traffickers as well. In 2013, Timothy Griesemer was charged with Commercial Sex Trafficking of a Child and Inducement of a Child to Engage in Prostitution in the small rural Midwestern farming town of Jerseyville, IL. "Griesemer attempted to recruit, induce, entice and obtain a child under the age of 14 years knowing that the person would be caused to be engaged in a commercial sex act" (US Attorney's Office, Southern District of Illinois,

2013). In fact, a third party "pimp," "madam," "bottom-girl," or "trafficker" is not needed in order to prosecute as a sex trafficking case. Buyers are being held accountable for these charges as well, when commercial sex involves minors (see Smith, et al., 2009). In contrast, buyers of prostituted adults involving force, fraud, or co-ercion have not yet been held accountable through sex trafficking charges. This is likely because it may be more difficult to prove that a buyer was aware that the survivor was trafficked as opposed to a willing sex worker, or that the focus of law enforcement centers upon trafficked minors.

Fraud

While described as uncommon, fraud was identified in at least one case involving two sex trafficking survivors social service providers worked with, as the victims of a false-front prostitution ring. A social service provider illustrated:

> We had one case where, it was really different, where it was a girl who she was being home schooled by her parents. Strong family unit, very active. And she was going to study abroad and when she got over there she found out it was a trafficking ring. And so now she is in a foreign country being trafficked and the family at some point realized that something was not right and that…. we've actually had two dads go over and rescue their daughters and he was one of them. And they were able to find them. Mmm hmmm, both of them. Very scary. One father had to pay off a rival pimp to find the location of his daughter …

The study abroad "trip" was really a front for a sex trafficking ring, in which the girls were redirected upon their arrival to a hotel where they fell under pimp control. Their travel documents were confiscated, they did not speak the language, and a pimp was at-tempting to force them into prostitution.

Parents As Traffickers

Another form of sex trafficking identified in the St. Louis bi-state area involved parents who sex-trafficked their children for drug money, or to pay off a drug debt. Social service providers and justice system professionals indicated that the prevalence of this practice was unknown, but known to occur in the St. Louis bi-state area. One individual working in the family courts stated:

> Then, for our kids, usually they have experienced some form of abuse or neglect in the home, which is I guess it is violence in the home ... it's usually a care-giver that's abusing or neglecting. We do see cases from time to time where our youth may be prostituted by a parent ...

One social service provider noted, "There are girls being rented out in their neighborhoods, even in churches, by a parent to get drugs or to pay for their drugs." Another social service provider stated, "And there's times you find that Moms are renting out their kids for drug money." This was described anecdotally to occur in largely rural Jefferson County, in relationship to methamphetamine, cocaine, and prescription pill use, and in St. Louis City, to support heroin addictions. Parents' selling their kids for drug money, or for survival, has been found in other research studies as well (Oselin, 2014; Raphael, 2010).

Child Pornography as Sex Trafficking

This chapter has to this point examined sex trafficking in the form of prostitution. Yet sex trafficking involves multiple forms of commercial sex. According to the Trafficking Victims Protection Act (TVPA), any commercial sex act involving a minor equates sex trafficking. Commercial sex acts take a variety of different forms, including pornography (Kotrla, 2010; MacKinnon, 2004; Nichols, 2015). When pornography is distributed for cash, traded for something of value, or is itself valuable, it is considered a form of commercial sex. Any situation where a minor is involved in pornography, regardless of whether the minor is forced, coerced, manipulated, or otherwise enticed into engaging in child pornography, is an act of sex trafficking.

In the Eastern District of Missouri, there were twelve federally prosecuted cases involving child pornography between January 2012 and May 2014. Seven of these cases involved possession of child pornography, and five more additionally involved the sexual exploitation of children to produce pornographic photos or videos. Approximately two-thirds of these occurred within 50 miles of St. Louis City (U.S. Attorney's Office, Eastern District of Missouri, 2014). In the Southern District of Illinois, there were thirty-four federally prosecuted cases in 2013 and 2104 involving child pornography. Twenty-four of these cases involved possession of child pornography, and ten more additionally involved the production of child pornography. Of these cases in the Southern District of Illinois, more than two-thirds occurred within 50 miles of St. Louis City (U.S. Attorney's Office, Southern District of Illinois, 2014).

One example of a child pornography case, which fits the legal definition of sex trafficking, occurred in Wood River, Illinois, a small river town just north of St. Louis. The case became notorious in the area largely due to the age of both the perpetrator and his victims. Seventy-one-year-old Charlie Jarrett was sentenced in 2013 to ten years in prison for distributing and possessing child pornography. An undercover investigation led to Jarrett's arrest and conviction. In 2012, the FBI found Jarrett used a peer-to-peer file sharing network, which allowed him to trade child pornography with other similar minded individuals. The investigation further uncovered thousands of images in Jarrett's home, on CD, in binders, and on his computer (US Attorney's Office, Southern District of Illinois, 2013). When men trade pornographic videos or images with one another through online sites, they are exchanging something of value—this constitutes a commercial sex act. In such circumstances involving minors, this automatically fits the legal definition of sex trafficking.

> US Attorney Wiggington stated, 'People need to know that there are men out there, like Mr. Jarrett and many others whom we have prosecuted, who join on-line worldwide

secret networks to view, distribute and exchange some of the most shocking and sickening videos and photographs of children, toddlers, and infants being raped. In this case our investigation found images and videos of adult males sexually penetrating infants and toddlers as well as toddlers forced to perform sexual acts on adults. Some of the images and videos included bondage and sadistic attacks on children' (US Attorney's Office, Southern District of Illinois, 2013).

Sex trafficking in the form of pornography, involving commercial sex acts with minors, occurs in the St. Louis area and surrounding regions in urban, rural, and suburban areas alike. From urban St. Louis City, to suburban neighborhoods in St. Charles, to small river towns like Wood River, IL, to the rural farming district of Dardenne Prairie, MO, the possession, production and distribution of child pornography occurs underground. It is possible that sex trafficking of adults for the purposes of pornography exists in the St. Louis bi-state area as well, but prosecuted cases were not found in the research, nor were cases identified by the criminal justice system or social services professionals who were interviewed for this research project.

In sum, the nature of sex trafficking manifested in multiple forms, including forced or coerced sex, deception, survival sex, a form of intimate partner violence, and child pornography. Trafficked prostitution was perpetrated by pimps, parents, friends, and boyfriends of adults, minors, males and females. The most common forms were the pimp-as-boyfriend and survival sex. Pimp-controlled prostitution without an intimate relationship was also a form of sex trafficking found in the St. Louis bi-state area, discussed in various parts of the chapter. In addition, parents sometimes sold their children for drug money, and in rare cases, individuals were defrauded into a sex trafficking situation. The types of sex trafficking victimization were multifaceted. Ostensibly, it is important to understand the risk factors that increase vulnerability to these diverse forms of sex trafficking.

Weak Social Institutions and Risk Factors of
Sex Trafficking Vulnerability

In the social sciences, a social institution is defined as a system reflecting multifaceted interrelated norms organized around a basic societal principle that meets basic and fundamental human needs. Education, economic, political, and healthcare systems, as well as religion and the family are commonly described in the field of sociology as social institutions. The social institutions examined in this section include the family, education systems, and facets of economic systems. Weak social institutions are associated with risk factors of sex trafficking. When weak social institutions are combined with weak social safety nets, those exposed to such social environments are susceptible to sex trafficking vulnerability. Social safety nets include things such as access to healthcare, unemployment or welfare benefits, and multiple social services. First, an unstable family life may lend itself to runaway or throwaway status; homeless youth may then become involved in a sex trafficking situation by either engaging in survival sex or getting involved with a boyfriend-as-pimp. Second, weak education systems increase the likelihood of truancy and drop-out status, increasing the potential for exposure to traffickers, who are actively looking for vulnerable or rebellious minors in the streets, walking in neighborhoods, sitting at bus stops, and frequenting parks and playgrounds. Third, economic conditions and the lack of social safety nets to address them are linked to sex trafficking vulnerability. Teen parents, those trying to support a family on a minimum wage salary, and those in poverty who have few resources for supporting themselves or their families may be more likely to fall into a trafficking situation. Lack of resources for substance abuse rehabilitation, economic and educational advancement, and services to assist women leaving prostitution also reflect a lack of social safety nets. Trafficked adults may find difficulty gaining employment due to a felony prostitution conviction on their records, resulting in a lack of options. Individuals who cannot access healthcare to address substance abuse or mental health issues are also vulnerable. The lack of social safety nets perpetuates current social and economic conditions conducive to sex trafficking vulnerability. Each of these is elaborated upon within the following subsections.

Home Life

A conflict-ridden home life may be related to sex trafficking victimization. Those who worked in the Juvenile Division of the Family Courts in St. Louis city, social service providers from three different organizations in St. Louis, and individuals working in the foster care system unanimously agreed that in the cases they worked with, problematic home lives were often a catalyst to sex trafficking victimization. At times, mothers' involvement in prostitution was related to their children becoming involved in prostitution. A social service provider indicated:

> I see this kind of generational domestic violence that also overlaps with prostitution and trafficking. So, what I mean by that is like, these kids are raised in a home where Mom is prostituted or prostituting but maybe she started at a very young age, so she at one point was a sex trafficking victim, and all of it's happening within the home, or she's bringing men in or maybe she leaves for a little bit, but it's definitely ... there's more often than not a domestic component to it.

Intergenerational transmission of prostitution is a little-explored area in the academic sex trafficking discourse. Yet, such findings have been presented in prior work, finding that when fathers are pimps and mothers are prostitutes, children may follow in their footsteps (Raphael & Myers-Powell, 2010; Oselin, 2014). In addition to parental involvement in prostitution, another social service provider indicated that abuse or neglect in the home was related to trafficking of minors; parents at times sex-trafficked their own children. Social service providers in foster care and those who directly worked with sex trafficking survivors noted that sometimes kids were pimped out by family members—even their own parents, usually to obtain or pay for drugs.

Another social service provider also described her experiences working with trafficked youth in the foster care system, who were in abusive or neglectful homes:

> What I'm seeing here in Missouri is I think younger girls getting into the trafficking world. I'm also seeing, and this could be because I work with trafficking survivors, but my main focus is I'm a specialized case worker through foster care. So, I work with children in foster care who have lengthy histories of being traumatized and being abused, of being abandoned by their biological families. So, oftentimes they are just looking to be loved. So, out of the girls that I've worked with ... they don't often recognize themselves as trafficking survivors because it was their boyfriend that introduced them, or this person loved them and they were doing favors for this person. So, I guess that's the majority of what I'm seeing ... that's how they're being introduced [into prostitution].

This abuse and neglect at home led to the risk of exploitation by a pimp professing love, affection, and caretaking. The director of the Juvenile Division of the family courts also delineated problematic home lives as a correlate of sex trafficking:

> And typically what we find, is that the home life is often in decay. There is a lot of conflict either with the mom or the mom's boyfriend, or something like that. And many of them are chronic runners. They run away a lot, and particularly for us, our concern is those that were runaways from foster-care ...

Another individual in the Juvenile Division also strongly felt, based upon his experiences working with trafficked girls in the justice system, that a conflicted home life was one of the major social influences on sex trafficking vulnerability. Conflict-ridden homes led to runaway status, truancy, and susceptibility to getting picked up by a pimp:

> I think mostly broken homes. Parent conflicts and.... we
> might see them in truancy where they are chronic run-
> ners, or we might see them where they come in and the
> police officers are like, at a loss for what to do with these
> kids and ... They call us ... And we're like, okay.... they
> are chronic runaways....

Those who worked in the justice system, foster care, and for homeless youth indicated problematic home lives were often at the root
of trafficking vulnerability, as such a home life led to runaway or
throwaway status, and consequent homelessness. Homeless youth
then had increased exposure to the pimps and buyers who were actively looking for them.

This dynamic was also present among LGBTQ youth. Several
social service providers indicated that lesbian, gay, bisexual, transgender, or queer youth were particularly vulnerable to a sex trafficking situation because of an increased likelihood of homelessness, largely due to conflict at home. Parents who did not accept
their children's LGBTQ identity either kicked their children out of
the house, or the child left willingly because of the hostile home
environment. When asked if she ever worked with LGBTQ survivors, one social service provider stated:

> Yeah, we do. Because sadly, there are higher rates of
> LGBTQ youth on the streets, if I have the statistic right,
> you know, like 30% of youth experience homelessness.
> But of the youth experiencing homelessness, like 40% of
> those identify as LGBTQ and a lot of that is because their
> parents don't want them in their homes, and they think
> that it is wrong, or they think that they have a moral or
> religious conflict with that. And so, these youth are really
> vulnerable, even more vulnerable because too, there aren't
> many services that are either A: culturally competent or
> B: there aren't many services specifically for, at least in the
> shelter sense, specifically for LGBTQ youth.

Ostensibly, in addition to runaway or throwaway status, vulnerability for LGBTQ youth may be heightened due to lack of services

specifically for, or clearly accepting, LGBTQ youth. This is described in more detail in Chapter 5.

Clearly, the research shows an association between problematic home lives and runaway or throwaway status, which are risk factors for sex trafficking victimization. Yet at times, respondents noted interacting with caring parents who were actively looking for their kids. For example, an individual in the Juvenile Division illustrated:

> Sometimes parents come in, we had a walk-in process where parents would come in and say my daughter runs away ... she's gone ... I don't know where she is ... I need some help. So then, we realized if this kid is running away and she's in Illinois or she's in Kansas City we know that it has something to do with sex ... like with what Dr. Lampley said, it is some man who cares about them ... some significant other who, under the premise of, I'm taking care of you, but then, there are kids channeling into sex trafficking.

Another group that specifically worked with sex-trafficked youth also indicated that at times, sex trafficking victims came from stable loving homes. For example, the director of The Covering House stated:

> Parents, believe it or not, when this first started I didn't think there were going to be parents involved, really caring and involved in these girls' lives, and they are, and we have had parents calling [for assistance], in addition to DJO's, case managers, and the courts.

So, while unstable or conflict ridden homes contributed to sex trafficking vulnerability, the presence of cases involving caring parents added another layer of complexity in understanding the broad spectrum of sex trafficking victimization. Home lives also overlapped with issues related to weak ties to education systems, which also facilitated truancy and increased exposure to pimps and traffickers.

Weak Education Systems: Truancy and Drop Outs

Weak education institutions and poor relationships with schools were also implicated in sex trafficking vulnerability in the St. Louis bi-state area. In particular, St. Louis City, some school districts in St. Louis County, and East St. Louis (IL.) are known for having some of the worst schools in the nation. Multiple school districts in the City, and in St. Louis County as well, had even lost their accreditation. Further, the student turnover rate is extremely high, with kids consistently moving from school district to school district (Crouch, 2013b). In fact, 36 schools had mobility rates higher that 50% in the St. Louis Public School system between 2011 and 2012 (Missouri Department of Elementary and Secondary Education, 2013). Poverty drives people from rental homes or apartments; when they cannot afford to pay the rent, they move, and often that means moving in and out of school districts. Moreover, teacher turnover is high as well, with a quarter of teachers in the St. Louis public school system leaving after the first year (Crouch, 2013a). St. Louis Public schools had a high school graduation rate of 45.9% in the 2013 school year, and a dropout rate of about 15% (Missouri Department of Elementary and Secondary Education, 2012, 2014). East St. Louis High School had fewer than three quarters of students graduate in 2011. Poverty, unstable living conditions, and weak education systems combine to produce sex trafficking vulnerability.

To elaborate, when kids have fewer ties to school and to education, and they are not at school and unsupervised during school hours, then they are more likely to be recruited by a pimp, as exposure is increased. The high drop-out rate and high truancy rate in some parts of the St. Louis metro area are related to vulnerability to sex trafficking. When asked if truancy was related to sex trafficking, Dr. Lampley, the director of the St. Louis City Juvenile Division responded:

> Oh yeah, because now they're out there with no skills, probably being influenced by those who are not in school or older, and I think that when kids have a connection to

school, I mean their outcomes are so much greater and we have a truancy unit here ... and some of our truancy officers have been dealing with some of these girls, and I know that we've learned that for girls that we are concerned that might be trafficked, certainly runaways, but very young 12, 13, 14 ... we just learned recently that we can go to the police department and they would draft a flyer of the missing girl, so if she's hanging in an area she looks like she's 18 because of the way that she's dressed and all of this, this is her age please contact us if you see her, that goes beyond the role of truancy, but our officers are very concerned and dedicated, they're going above and beyond to try and help some of these girls.

Another individual in the Juvenile Division of the Family Courts stated:

I think with school, you know, they spend six hours a day at school, so if they are not at school that is six hours of free time to be on Back Page or Viva dot com or wherever else, so I think school occupies a lot of their time, but if they are not there ...

Another social service provider and survivor indicated how LGBTQ identities could be related to an increased likelihood of truancy, and how this then increased the risk of trafficking victimization:

I think one of the things that I think is really critical with LGBTQ youth who are disenfranchised, who are probably in survival mode, might be on the streets ... because one of the things that I share at my trainings is 1/3rd of LGBTQ youth miss school one or more days in a month for feeling unsafe. So if you have 1/3rd of these youth who are out missing school, where are they? Best-case scenario is that they are at home playing Wii, that's the best-case scenario. Worst-case scenario is what? So if they're not in school, so then I always ask adults, I'm like, what are the consequences of a young person missing school? Lower graduation rates, poor tests scores, dropout, getting placed in alternative spaces, not being in school period! So if they're not in school then where are they? They're probably in places like the detention center. They're in like alternative treatment centers. They're in residential treatment centers. They're on the streets. So, they're engaged in sex work. They're being trafficked, that's what's happening to them.

This survivor noted that the dynamic of missing school and living on the streets impacted his own involvement with sex trafficking, in the form of survival sex as a homeless and truant gay-identified youth. The director of the Juvenile Division, Dr. Lampley, further noted that chronic truancy could be an identification point for potential sex trafficking victims:

That's actually how we had a transfer case from another jurisdiction, that's how it came to us, because it was a … but because how it came to the court in another jurisdiction because a girl had chronic absences from school. And then, we kept digging, and digging, and kept digging and realized that she's being trafficked, but in her mind she wanted to be out there. Mom actually did not enforce her going to school, and we find that for a number of reasons, but if mom is at work and allowing her to stay home or stay home and care for younger siblings she's not really aware that all of these other things are going on.

As illustrated in this example, poverty and truancy may be intertwined. As there are few social safety nets available to lower class families, at times, older children may stay home from school to take care of younger children so parents can work. This example also delineates that a lack of resources for daycare provision to poor families produces an environment that may increase risk of sex trafficking. Further, this example is representative of multiple statements of social service providers and justice system professionals that truancy is a potential indicator of sex trafficking risk.

In sum, those working in the family courts and in social services found that truancy or drop-out status was a risk factor for sex trafficking victimization, largely due to increased unsupervised time and increased exposure to pimps and buyers. In addition, if an individual does not have a high level of education, s/he is more likely to be in poverty. There are multiple factors associated with poverty and sex trafficking vulnerability.

Poverty

Lack of economic resources is tied to weak education institutions, but it is also tied to survival sex as well as increased risk of sex trafficking. While the authors recognize that some women and men engage in sex work as an occupation of choice, sex work can at times evolve into a sex trafficking situation. In several prosecuted cases of sex trafficking in the area, women may have initially agreed to engage in sex work in partnership with a pimp to improve their economic positions, but the situation shifted, in which their money was confiscated, they were subjected to violence, and not allowed to leave the trade. For example, in St. Charles County, a suburban area of the Metro St. Louis area, officers received an anonymous call about a suspicious situation occurring at the Red Roof Inn. Two adult teenagers, one eighteen and the other nineteen, had both initially agreed to engage in sex work as single parents working to make ends meet. Coercion, verbal abuse, and force were found to be involved in this case. The St. Charles County prosecutor described the girls to a local news agency as "easy prey" who were "strapped for cash" and were "struggling to feed their babies" (Fazal, 2013). Michael Johnson and Samantha Ginochhio were charged with sex trafficking. Samantha was responsible for arranging the "dates," hotels, and payment while Michael received the money. Michael initially recruited one of the survivors at a restaurant, indicating that she could be making a lot more money than in the restaurant. While both girls initially agreed to the sex work, they were not allowed to stop, and threatened with physical harm when they wanted to quit. Accordingly, sex work developed quickly into a sex trafficking situation, as Samantha and Michael would not allow them to stop prostituting. There were multiple prosecuted cases in the bi-state area involving this dynamic of sex-work turned sex-trafficking. In addition, it should be noted that the adult teens were making a socially conditioned choice to engage in sex work, impacted by their identities as low wage-earning single parents. Some individuals choose sex work as an occupation they enjoy; yet others engage in sex work primarily to get out of poverty, and in many cases, even for daily survival.

Further, lack of available resources for adults in prostitution intertwined with poverty may work to reproduce survival sex situations. One social service provider used an example to illustrate, working with a woman who was prostituted by her boyfriend for a number of years who had difficulty finding the means of supporting herself and her children:

> What I'm finding with someone like her is that she doesn't have any marketable job skills. So, even if she were to find a position, she also has felony convictions on her record that preclude her from working with a lot of organizations and companies. So, I see a lot of giving up, and contemplating going back into the lifestyle in order to survive, because they can't … they can't get legitimate employment …

Trafficked adults may find difficulty gaining employment for having a felony prostitution conviction on their records, or cannot access food stamps or welfare for the same reason, increasing the likelihood of being re-trafficked, or in some cases, even becoming traffickers themselves. A social service provider stated:

> Yeah. They're called 'the bottom girl,' yeah. So they'll be either aged out, which is about 25, is when they're considered no longer useful, and then, they become the perpetrator, because honestly where do you go? What do you put on a resume at that point? And then, they've been in that situation for so long.

Further, trying to pay for a prostitution fine with little access to legitimate employment works to reproduce the "revolving door" into prostitution-as-survival sex as well. One survivor explained:

> ... the prostitute gets fined $1,000 and then by golly she can't make it, how do you think she is going to make that money? She is going to go out and turn a trick!

Ironically, misguided criminal justice policy, intended to deter prostitution, actually functioned to reproduce it. This dynamic overlapped with mental health and substance abuse issues as well.

Mental Health & Substance Abuse

Several social service providers indicated that a lack of resources for those suffering from serious mental illness and substance abuse issues was problematic in that it increased the likelihood of becoming involved in survival sex. In fact, such issues were related to sexual exploitation and sex trafficking, as fewer options for employment were available to those with these ailments. When asked what provided challenges to service provision for sex-trafficking survivors, an individual working in the juvenile courts stated, "Sometimes we find that there are some mental health issues that, I mean, that have to be addressed ..." When asked for an example, he replied:

> She was bipolar. So some of these undiagnosed mental illness so with the drugs the alcohol on top of the mental health ... make it even bigger.... sometimes the family is all tied into it also, the family never [could] get mental help treatment for this young child. So then it grows into that.

The same individual went on to describe how untreated mental illness was at times interrelated with problems in school and truancy, which increased the risk of trafficking victimization:

> I think there are some family dysfunction, lack of parental supervision and control and sometimes some of these kids are having school problems, and I think that even stems

from the mental health issues, these kids are truant. Problems at school and peer interaction may get in the way.... so I think it's a combination of different issues, but I think the mental health part is foremost.

A social service provider elaborated, by providing a description of how drug abuse and mental illness were intertwined, and associated with survival sex. He indicated that it was difficult for individuals to hold jobs when they had substance abuse and mental health issues. They then became vulnerable to sexual exploitation, as they needed to support their drug habits to self-medicate to address their mental illness. His example illustrates such dynamics:

Another person [client] he had a really major drug problem and also had a major mental illness I think, at least bi-polar and personality disorder as well and he kind of got pulled into another situation where he was living with a guy who he would provide sexual services for in exchange for a place to live and drugs.

Ostensibly, survival sex could be influenced by weak social institutions, in the form of lack of drug rehabilitation centers and reduced access to mental healthcare. For example, one respondent noted:

Our stumbling block in St. Louis, specifically, because that's what I've dealt with, would be the system. It's the welfare system. It's the drug rehabilitation availability, especially heroin. It's the system.

When asked for an example, she stated:

I have several ... a good one is we find, and I'm using a specific case: so we find a girl on the street. She asks for help. She is addicted to heroin. I cannot take her to a shelter while she is addicted. I cannot take her to a drug rehabilitation center because there are no beds available that minute; because of the trauma bonds and the PTSD and just the general Stockholm Syndrome they're suffering, I don't have two or three days to come back to them, find them again and hope that they will be there and ready for help. If they are ready for help I have to go right now, and I can't get a girl into a heroin bed at a drop of a finger.

Accordingly, in access to substance abuse rehabilitation was noted as problematic, and this dynamic contributed to the perpetuation of sex trafficking, both in preventing recovery and in recreating a social environment in which prostitution to meet drug and survival needs was more or less inevitable. This dynamic is conflated with in access to welfare and food stamps in the state of Missouri for those with a drug felony. "It's already hard to get a job as a felon, but no access to cash assistance or food stamps makes it even more difficult to secure the basics in order to find a job and get back on one's feet. Many drug felons have drug addictions and need to use treatment centers. However, treatment centers have long depended on TANF and SNAP programs to offset the costs of their own programs. No benefits means higher costs for drug treatment, which means fewer people can get help" (Downs, 2013). Denial of safety nets—food stamps, welfare, mental health and substance abuse programs—reinforces the revolving door back into prostitution by reducing opportunities for recovery and upward mobility.

In sum, the dynamics that contribute to vulnerability to sex trafficking or sexual exploitation include weak social institutions, such as poor education systems, failure to provide a minimum wage as a living wage (particularly for single teen parents), lack of affordable daycare resources, limited access to mental health or substance abuse rehabilitation, services for those leaving prostitution, misguided criminal justice policy, and conflict-ridden families. This lays the foundation for traffickers to traffic or exploit vulnerable youth and adults, who use a variety of techniques to do so.

Techniques of Traffickers

The techniques that traffickers use are multifaceted, and include efforts toward recruitment, presenting barriers to leaving, and conducting trafficking operations. The primary aim of the trafficker is to make money, and to reduce the risk of getting caught. The following subsections highlight recruiting individuals into sex trafficking operations, as well as presenting various forms of abuse that serve as barriers to sex trafficking survivors' ability to leave the situation. Last, the ways sex trafficking operations are conducted, through use of the Internet, hotels, and interstate circuits are detailed.

Recruitment

As indicated above, various weakened social institutions produce social environments conducive to sex trafficking vulnerability. Pimps actively seek out homeless, runaway, or throwaway youth, as well as disabled, economically or socially marginalized people, and those who are frequently truant or otherwise rebellious, or have unstable home lives. Social service providers, justice system officials, and survivors noted that involvement in the sex industry often started with pimps looking for women, girls, men, and boys in vulnerable positions. As one survivor pointed out:

> As long as we have these men paying for sex, guys are going to go out and look for vulnerable teenagers. They are going to look for vulnerable working waitresses in little places that are poor and they are going to look for victims, women that are vulnerable, boys that are vulnerable, men that are vulnerable, they are going to look for vulnerable human beings, that they can make a financial gain off.

Another survivor elaborated on the techniques of traffickers she had been in contact with, indicating what a typical approach looked like:

> Traffickers are going to be at a bus stop looking for that lost soul that looks like there is nobody else there and say, 'Hey! You need a ride? What's going on? What's your name? Can I buy you....' You know what I'm saying, and

they are going to befriend them. That's a lot more how this looks ...

A social service provider who worked with homeless or troubled youth specifically indicated the vulnerability of homeless youth to pimp control:

But a lot of times what we see are youth that have ended up on the streets for some reason, and need a place to stay, they need food, they need belonging, even. And so, a lot of times pimps and traffickers prey on that, and end up forming relationships with these youth. I've seen youth prostituted out of car washes. I have seen them have boyfriends and girlfriends, even that they really do love and care about, but are selling them at the same time, maybe it's to get drug money. A lot of times there seems to be some overlap there, or maybe it's just so that they have money to take care of themselves. And so, it's really, really common whether you put that as survivor sex, transactional sex, but really it is technically sex trafficking under that definition. And so, as far as numbers go, it's hard to say ... but I feel like probably over half of my case-load have experienced it to some extent, and usually multiple forms and types and times it has occurred.

Further, traffickers looked to fulfill whatever need an individual had, whether it was economic or emotional, or for basic survival. As one social service provider illustrated:

So if they need physical needs met, then it's I'll buy this for you if you do this.... if it's the dad figure, then I just become a dad figure. If they need a boyfriend, or if they want a boyfriend ... then I become the perfect boyfriend. And girls will put on their statuses [on social media] what they're looking for in a perfect boyfriend so it makes it easier. So they can just become that role, and so that is the scary part is that even the way that I've done my statuses the past two years have changed. Albeit mine is private, just knowing that it's so easy to put information out there that it just gives me … it tells me who you are or what you need and then they can use that for grooming I think … like you hear all the time it's business if you hear traffickers talk that it's business so I just find what I need and then, they fill the hole that kid needs. So if it's she needs to feel pretty then I tell her that she's pretty.

Traffickers recruitment strategies were adaptable to the situation at hand, and they could play the role of a boyfriend, "daddy," or whatever it was perceived that the victim needed emotionally or physically. Once this trust and relationship was established, and then the psychological abuses evolved and continued, typically with the addition of physical, economic, and sexual abuses. Recruitment distinctly played upon vulnerabilities.

LGBTQ Identities

The recruitment of LGBTQ kids and young adults may be somewhat unique. According to survivors and social service providers, LGBTQ youth were susceptible to sex trafficking, as traffickers may exploit the desire to explore sexuality and sexual orientation. Youth were interested in same-sex interactions, and traffickers were there to make a profit from it. A social service provider who worked in the foster care system described a case with a survivor she worked with:

Yeah he was a young man, he was actually born in somewhere in Russia or like Eastern Europe, and immigrated here with this parents. He was abandoned in a hotel when he was like 11, was very street savvy, I got his case when he was 20, and he ages out of the system at 21. He was battling his sexuality, as far as, he was in a very religious foster home who told him that he was sinning, that he was going to hell, and all of that stupid shit! … I'm still in touch with him now … I haven't had his case for a year or two but he's doing really well … he's recognizing why he was forced to do that, and why he accepted, and why at the time he did not feel forced. His situation was unique in that it was presented to him as a way to explore his sexuality. So he was being told especially of the Eastern European descent that being gay was very wrong to him. So, he thought by being told to be on the street to make this person money, that he was exploring if he really was gay or not, because he was engaging in same-sex sex acts. So that's kind of the way that he phrased it in his head, but he certainly saw that he was victimized and that of course that wasn't a healthy way to do it, and he was being taken advantage of.

While such individuals could have been guided into an exploration of sexuality without sex work, or explored same-sex relationships themselves, or even engaged in sex work without someone else making money from it, instead youth were guided into exploitive situations in which they made money for someone else.

Another social service provider indicated that while safe spaces and subcultures that provided family, mentorship, and guidance were present in St. Louis, there were other spaces that were exploitive of LGBTQ youth:

In the African American community there's this sort of subculture within mostly the gay community, called the 'Ball Culture' not like a Cinderella Ball, but more like a Vogueing Ball. There is this whole sort of like, there's houses. So a house would be kind of like a family, where let's say you're kicked out by your own biological family, you might, sometimes it's a physical house where you would go stay, and where it's kind of like this family where people sort of create, like it's usually, they say it's a matriarchal system because there is usually like a drag queen or a transgender woman who is sort of mother of the house, and everyone takes her last name which is usually a name after like a fashion designer or a fancy car or something like that. So, anyway there would be all of these folks living together or sometimes, not necessarily living together but forming close-knit families and kind of ... and then they have these events where the different houses will compete against each other and they will have different categories of different styles of vogueing and dancing and those kinds of things. It's really interesting subculture and I think that I've met some folks for whom it was a life-saving thing, where they met mentors and support and found guidance and found somebody who actually took them in and provided basic things for them. Some of them have actually gone on to go to college and do interesting things. And so, I think some of the houses are pretty good, they are pretty healthy and good. I also know of some situations where there's some, I don't know if you would call it sex work, or sex trafficking exactly, but it's sort of has you've got these young kids usually who have just come out of the closet and sometimes are kicked out by their families and then they're taken in by older people in this community and not all of those older people are necessarily healthy influences, in terms of substance abuse or … and sometimes it's hard to tell how much of the … certainly, in some of the houses, sex that is happening between these younger people and these older people, or between lots of different people and whether there is exploitation going on there is sometimes hard to pick out. But I think certainly there have been situations where I felt like it was exploitationı

When asked for an example, he elaborated:

Just a young kid who had been kicked out of their home and was looking for a community, looking for friends, looking for a new family and found it, but was really young, and had the adults that were supposed to be like the new family were introducing the client to a lot high risk things and, in terms of, risky sexual stuff, sex work, and also drugs, those were the main things, I guess …

Another social service provider, who is also gay and a survivor of sex trafficking, indicated that buyers-as-traffickers even trolled local centers where LGBTQ youth are known to frequent. Safe spaces for LGBTQ youth were described as problematic by some respondents, both on the street and even in social services. In addition to LGBTQ identities, and unique vulnerabilities to recruitment, disability status also impacted susceptibility to sex trafficking recruitment.

Disability

One example involving exploiting a mentally disabled woman involved brother-sister duo Carla and Carl Mathews. Carla, also known by the self-given nickname "Black Barbie" for her Barbie-doll like appearance, was a prostitute herself. The pair worked to prostitute two women in Breckenridge Hills, a St. Louis County lower working class neighborhood. One of the women they trafficked had mental disabilities, and the Mathews deceived her into believing that she had to sell sex in order to access food stamps. Carl and Carla took food stamp cards away from both of the women they trafficked as a way to control them, and also gave them the drug MDMA, more commonly known as ecstasy, before sending them to clients. The Mathews also withheld food and drinks to control them as well. Carla was believed to have set up the encounters with clients, including reserving a hotel room, driving the women to the hotel, collecting the money. Carl was involved in aiding Carla with setting up the "dates." He admitted to physically abusing the mentally disabled woman, and also threatened to kill her. Carl even video-recorded the disabled woman being beaten by another woman. The disabled woman was forced to eat, sleep, and go to the bathroom in the closet.

Carl initially recruited the disabled woman when she was a minor in the foster care system. Carl befriended her, and she was forced to leave her foster home because Carl was a convicted sex offender and she continued to see him. Carl had previously served five years for raping a ten-year-old girl when he was seventeen. After being forced to leave, the woman moved in with Carl and Carla. The second victim was also held captive by the Mathews. She lived with them at a motel in Bridgeton, near the St. Louis airport. She was forced to sell sex to men in the motel and give the money to the Mathews. When she tried to escape, Carl chased her down and beat her. The case was discovered when a visitor to the Mathews' apartment found a naked woman crammed below the bottom shelf of a closet, who appeared to have physical injuries. When police were contacted, they found multiple burns on the woman's back, thighs, arms, and shoulders. They also found her with two black eyes from an apparent beating. Both Carl and Carla were sentenced to ten years for conspiring to commit sex trafficking. It is likely that the pair chose a mentally disabled woman as their victim because she was easier to control.

In sum, targeting the homeless, runaways, throwaways, the disabled, LGBTQ youth or adults may involve the trafficker posing as a friend, or as a romantic partner. At times, the relationships may function similarly to an intimate partner violence relationship, or in what appears to be the start of a friendship. The trafficker may express caring and concern, or act as a father figure, friend, mentor, or boyfriend, who later turns into a controlling abuser. The abuse may manifest psychologically and physically, with threats, manipulation, physical abuse, and/or coercion. These forms of abuse serve as barriers to prevent the sex trafficking victim from leaving the trafficker.

Barriers to Leaving

Barriers to leaving are put in place purposefully by traffickers. Traffickers may use psychological or emotional abuse to control the sex trafficking survivors. As one survivor, "Marion," poignantly stated based on her experiences:

> A bad guy is going to *look* like a really great guy so he can *be* that bad guy; because it's going to work in his favor more. He's going to have more control, he's going to have more power. He's going to have that emotional connection. You're going to have that emotional connection, that emotional bond, and they're going to have a lot more power. They can spend a lot of time invested in building that trust.

This illustrated how the "boyfriend" pimp engaged in psychological abuses. "Marion" noted that pimps typically worked to gain trust and emotional attachments of the women and girls they aimed to engage in prostitution. This kept victims disconnected from labeling themselves as victims, and served as a barrier to leaving. She stated:

> A bad guy is going to not look like a bad guy to do bad stuff. He's going to look like a really great guy, because he's going to get a lot further if he earns your trust. He's going to have you in a more vulnerable position, then, he's going to have your emotional control.

Barriers to leaving "the life" also resulted from pimp-coercion involving "telling" the parents. For example another survivor stated:

> Because when you're 16 how do you call your mom? Oh especially if … and if you have your pimp or boyfriend yeah…. I'm going to tell them you've been a prostitute. Then, you know what? You have to stand in that judgment. Well, you already have guilt and shame because that's just a terrible blow to the ego, the esteem, I mean everything.

Consequently, in such cases, the fear and shame in telling the parents about things the survivors had already done influenced survivors to continue selling sex as a form of coerced sex trafficking, preventing them from leaving "the life."

Victims may not identify themselves as trafficking victims for a variety of different reasons. For some, they may engage in self-blame, seeing themselves as the cause of their harm rather than those around them. Some will still be so attached to their pimps, boyfriends, or clients that they see themselves as responsible, although they are "doing it for him." Moreover, they may be unaware of what trafficking is, for example, a social service provider stated, "Well, and the other thing, the victim isn't gonna say, 'I'm a victim of human trafficking'… I mean they are not even going to know what that means." A legal advocate elaborated:

The other thing we alert people to is that, it's typical for a trafficking victim not to realize that they are a trafficking victim. Sometimes they just think they were stupid and so, they got themselves into this mess, or they should have known better, this kind of thing. They think they're in rough circumstances, but they don't even realize that it is criminal circumstances ...

A survivor expanded on self-blame and victimization-disconnect, by providing a personal account of self-blame, preventing her initial recognition of herself as a victim, which also prevented her help-seeking:

But once that happens it's that guilt and shame, it's too much for you to be able to do anything about it, especially when you're young. What do you do, raise up your head and say, 'Mom, guess what? Somebody just paid to have sex with me!' Really??! Because then you're questioning your judgment call, 'How did, how could I have gotten to this point? How could I have let this person' — and then, at the same time you're thinking, 'Oh my God, I love him [the 'boyfriend' pimp].'

This case exemplifies both the psychological bond to the pimp, tying this survivor to a trafficking situation, and also the guilt and shame that prevented her from returning to her Mom. When it is perceived that there is nowhere to go because of non-acceptance, while simultaneously loving an abusive pimp who does provide acceptance, these things intersect to prevent leaving the situation. This survivor further elaborated on the guilt and shame, when asked, "So you're saying the guilt and the shame keeps you in the life longer?"

It can keep you prisoner, yes. Absolutely! And that's one of the first things that I tell people, you have to let go of the guilt and shame or you're never going to, it's the only way that you can move on. Because that's going to be the worst thing to hold you back is that guilt and shame, guilt

and shame of all of the ugly things … yes the guilt and
shame is just awful.

Accordingly, living in a world in which prostitution is largely stigmatized creates an atmosphere of non-acceptance of those involved in prostitution, which ironically, may prevent trafficked
people from leaving sex trafficking situations.

In addition to psychological abuses, physical abuse accompanied many sex trafficking cases. Perhaps most notorious in the St.
Louis area is the case of Carl and Carla Mathews, described above.
Beating, hitting, broken bones, burns, and withholding food were
described as tools of control and coercion of traffickers. Richard
Anderson was found to have broken the nose of one of his victims,
a young teen adult. Jamal Brown also broke the nose of one of his
victims, who was discovered due to her hospitalization for the broken nose and other physical abuses. In addition to psychological
and physical abuses, trafficking operations worked to build barriers
to leaving, simply through reduced likelihood of identification.

Trafficking Operations

The Internet

Use of the Internet has been implicated as a common way of
both recruiting victims and advertising to clients. In Florissant, a
St. Louis County suburb, three teenage girls, including two minors, were sex trafficked by a male pimp, Anton Morris, thirty-
nine years old. The teens, seventeen and nineteen, escaped
through a bedroom window while the pimp was sleeping, and contacted police, who later got the sixteen-year-old out of the home.
Morris was charged with two counts of sexual trafficking of a child
for the trafficking of the sixteen- and seventeen-year-old, and one
count of trafficking for the purposes of sexual exploitation for the
nineteen-year-old. Morris initially recruited the sixteen-year-old
on Facebook, posing as her friend. The teens were sold on multiple

sites online, and met buyers at hotels in the area. He even coerced one victim into recruiting the other girls.

The case of Richard Anderson also illustrates how the Internet can be used to advertise victims to buyers. Richard Anderson, a twenty-three-year-old man living in Cahokia, IL, a small city in the St. Louis Metro East area, was sentenced for enticing a minor into prostitution. The case was uncovered by the St. Louis County Police Department's Special Investigations Unit, which was conducting an undercover operation in the summer of 2012 to work to identify minors trafficked online in the St. Louis area. Backpage.com's escort section is widely regarded as a top site for offering sexual services. It is unknown how many of these ads represent trafficked individuals. The advertisement that Anderson posted on Backpage.com stated the girl depicted in the ad was 19, and an out-of-state area code was listed. These two dynamics are both red flags for investigators, who sometimes monitor Internet ads that sell sex and conduct sting operations. The girl was later found by investigators to be seventeen years old. Anderson posted the ads of the teen, and kept all of her earnings. Anderson was also found to have perpetrated emotional and physical abuse toward the girl, including punching her in the face and breaking her nose. He also held her ID. Anderson was sentenced to just over five years in prison by a federal court. This prosecuted case offers one, among many, of sex trafficking cases in which traffickers use the Internet to sell victims.

In addition to prosecuted cases, social service providers also reported that their clients, about half, had been trafficked on the Internet through personal ads, Facebook, and more.

> Yeah. We are seeing ... I would say right now if I had just to guess what statistics there probably would be half and half. I think last year a lot more of our cases were probably internet. Dedee and I had experienced one of our first cases, was actually from out of state, when a family contacted us and we within 20 minutes were able to find their daughter on that page. It was just that easy, just from knowing what she looked like, what city we thought she

would be in ... and so, it was a very quick, like too quick, and too easy, like we shouldn't have been able to find her that easy. We're seeing a lot of girls that have had a sexual trauma and then at 13 and 14 they will put their own personal ads there, online and their response is well, at least I can control what happens to me, or their boyfriends will do it as personal ads. A lot of things are happening over social media, iPhones, it's real easy for kids to proposition other kids, or proposition, here's my girlfriend, here's my ... look what you could have ... Facebook is an easy one just ... I'm not very tech-savvy so Facebook because I only have to get one girl to friend me, and then, I have access to her two or three hundred other friends and it's easy for me ... then they can just go through the statuses and see who they think would be easy to groom. So it just makes it a lot easier and a lot more hidden I think too.

Respondents further elaborated on the ways in which traffickers embedded messages in their advertisements. While they did not usually directly advertise an exchange of sex for money, traffickers used language stating that the women and girls pictured in the advertisements wanted to have sex, and used codes for the expected payment of sexual services. Moreover, respondents indicated use of specialized codes specifically for underage girls. For example, a social service provider stated:

And there are certain code things that they put in those things like 'young,' 'new,' 'fresh to the scene,' 'cheerleader,' 'princess,' they use kind of these younger terms as code. And then they also price it out. They won't say 80 dollars, they'll say 80 hugs, 80 stars, 80 hearts—and that's the code.

In addition to social service providers' discussions of Internet solicitation, the federal prosecutor who participated in the current study also described traffickers' use of the Internet. As an example of entrée into online solicitation, a former federal prosecutor, now a judge, delineated that in a recently prosecuted case of domestic trafficking, the trafficker found a victim in vulnerable circumstances, and she shortly became a trafficking victim:

> In this instance, there was not much evidence of physical violence, but certainly other forms of manipulation and coercion knowing that our victim was pretty much on the street in pajamas when they picked her up. Invited her back to their house, and within a few days they had put her on the internet and advertised her services for prostitution. They ended up here in St. Louis because they ran a circuit between Minneapolis and lots of other cities in the Midwest, and St. Louis is common destination on the circuit—and through a bunch of other things that I really can't get into—we ended up catching them here.

Respondents indicated victims entered into a trafficking situation when pimps found them in vulnerable circumstances. The present study also found that following an initial encounter with a pimp, some victims were soon advertised on the Internet. In fact, multiple interviewees in the justice system and social services indicated that the Internet was a common way of selling sex. Another social service provider described a case involving a mentally disabled young adult being trafficked on the Internet:

> We had a case early on when 'Lucy' first came here where she got a call from a close friend from Arkansas whose older daughter, I think she was maybe 19, the mother knew that she was being trafficked, but she had some mental disabilities and so she was maybe 13 or 14 in her mental capacities, and so, we talked to the mother, she was beside herself, and we said, 'Can you give us any information?' She knew the town and so I said okay. So what we did was we got online, we went to the backpage, because that's the go-to place, (snapping fingers) I started looking through, boom! Pulled this one, and 'Lucy' said, 'That's her.' Then we found her within no time.

In fact, there were several cases in which parents found their own children advertising sex online, and sought out assistance to recover them. Another social service provider illustrated:

> The Back Page is the new go-to place. It's a very common place for pimps. We had a girl who was rescued by her dad and she was being ... they were trying to force her to go onto the Back Page and she resisted and resisted, she had some physical abuse because of it, like cigarette burns that had been put out on her ...

In a federal prosecuted case in the Eastern District of Missouri, Twenty-five-year-old Maurice Dontae Alexander recruited a sixteen-year-old teen runaway for his sex trafficking operation, along with partner Latoshia Norris, also 25. The pair were from Minneapolis, and invited the runaway into their home, giving her food, clothing, shelter, and a job in prostitution. They advertised her sexual services on Backpage.com, and ran an Internet circuit between Des Moines, Iowa, the Kansas City area, and Indianapolis, advertising her in different cities at different points in time. They were both charged with enticement of a minor to engage in prostitution, and likely will face a six-year sentence. This example depicts both use of the Internet in trafficking operations, as well as use of interstate circuits. Interstate circuits are described in more detail below.

Interstate Circuits

As in the case described above, respondents illustrated traffickers' use of "circuits," or interstate movement of trafficking victims. In many of the cases that were discussed in the interviews, traffickers not only used the Internet for recruitment and solicitation, but also moved victims from city to city to avoid getting caught or attracting too much attention. In fact, solicitations for the same victim would appear online in multiple cities at different points in time, following what social service providers and the federal prosecutor described as "running the circuit." In such cases, where traffickers are constantly moving the victims, it is difficult to track them (see Chapter 4).

Sex trafficking related charges include transporting for the purposes of prostitution, which appear in some federally prosecuted cases in the St. Louis area. In Hazelwood, a working and middle class northern suburb of St. Louis, Barry Wimberly received nearly five years in prison, with lifetime supervision following his release, for transporting five women from five different states, including Missouri, for the purposes of prostitution. Wimberly used interstate circuits to move the women between Missouri, Illinois, North Dakota, Minnesota, Georgia and Florida. Similarly, in 2014 Jamall Brown was also sentenced to just over four years in prison on charges of transporting for the purposes of prostitution, with supervision for life upon release. He moved two women between Chicago, Missouri, and Colorado to sell them for sex. The case was uncovered at a St. Louis hospital, where one of the women sought treatment for a broken nose and other injuries perpetrated by Brown. She initially met Brown in their hometown of Chicago through a friend. She reported Brown assaulted her and her friend, who Brown also trafficked. Brown forced both women to advertise themselves on Backpage.com to sell sex. A few days after their initial meeting in Chicago, Brown took them to St. Louis, and then moved them to Denver, and back to St. Louis for the purposes of prostitution. When the first victim told Brown she wanted to leave, and did not want to prostitute, Brown beat her and fractured her nose. He dropped her off at a St. Louis hospital, where police were called and convinced her to press charges. This case indicates both the use of interstate circuits, and movement that can accompany some trafficking cases. The case also further illustrates a situation where victims may initially consent to prostitution, but then they are physically assaulted when they try to leave and forced to continue.

In yet another case involving interstate movement, in 2014 Reginald Williams was convicted on multiple charges of transporting two minors with the intent to engage in prostitution. In 2012 in Collinsville, Illinois, in the St. Louis Metro East area, a report for a missing girl, sixteen years old, who was reported to be forced to prostitute by one or more adult men. The person reporting the crime found the missing girl on Backpage.com, where she was advertised as a twenty-year-old woman offering sexual services. Police were able to trace the phone number in the ad to Reginald Williams. Investigators also found that another girl was involved, and they were residing at a St. Louis County hotel; at that point, the FBI and St. Louis County Police became involved. An undercover detective responded to the Backpage ad, and set up a "date" with the girls. At the hotel, they saw Williams leave the room, and he was arrested shortly after. The other girl was seventeen, and was also offered on Backpage.com. The investigators discovered that Williams moved the girls from Chicago to St. Louis to sell them for sex. In addition to interstate transportation of a minor for the purposes of prostitution, Williams was also convicted of sex trafficking of a minor, and attempted sex trafficking of a minor, among other charges.

Chapter Summary

In conclusion, sex trafficking in the St. Louis bi-state area was found to be multifaceted and complex. Sex trafficking took the forms of both child pornography and prostitution. In child pornography cases, creating, distributing/trading, and possessing child pornography could all be viewed as sex trafficking victimization. Creating child pornography is an act of sex trafficking, as it involves the creation of something of value involving the sexual exploitation of a minor. Distributing child pornography often entails trading it for other images, or getting an "in" in online trading forums, holding commercial value involving the sexual exploitation of children. Possessing child pornography creates the demand for its continued production, serving as a catalyst to sex trafficking. Prostitution was the most common form of sex trafficking found in St. Louis. Individuals from rural, suburban, and inner-city communities encompassing varied race, culture, sex, sexual orientation, and gender identities experienced sex trafficking victimization. African American girls were overrepresented in prosecuted cases. Weak social institutions, such as poor education systems, conflict-ridden families, and weak economic systems combined with inadequate social safety nets, created a social environment conducive to sex trafficking vulnerability. This vulnerability served to increase the risk of getting involved with a pimp, or being sexually exploited by buyers. Boyfriends romancing girls and then pimping them out was the most common form of sex trafficking found in the St. Louis bi-state area, along with survival sex and consequent sexual exploitation by pimps and buyers. However, parents trafficking their own children for drug money, as well as fraud, were also implicated in sex trafficking victimization. Traffickers used the Internet, as well as interstate movement, and a variety of physical and emotional abuses to conduct their operations. Small scale operations, usually controlled by a pimp or a pimp with a partner, or sexual exploitation by buyers of vulnerable youth were most common, as opposed to organized crime rings found in other locations. In sum, sex trafficking in the St. Louis bi-state area was found to be complex, multifaceted, and involved multiple shades of grey. Vulnerability as runaways, truants, poor home lives, disability, LGBTQ status, and poverty intersected to create an environment prime for traffickers and buyers to exploit youth and adults.

Chapter 4

Policing Human Trafficking

Whether it is online or by patrol, in the office, on the street, or in the courtroom, legal officials, local and federal, as well as at all inter-departmental stages, have the burdensome task of investigating and prosecuting human trafficking offenders. Not only do the actors in the legal arena have to identify perpetrators and potential victims, but they must also provide evidence that proves beyond a reasonable doubt that the charge meets the core legal components of human trafficking. Federally, policing agents must provide evidence that the act, whether it is sexual or labor oriented, occurred because of force, fraud, or coercion, with the exception of cases involving the commercial sexual exploitation of a minor. This "means" element has proven to be the most difficult to establish, and thereby, forces prosecutors and police to charge the offender with a lesser offense so that some punishment is incurred. Because human trafficking cases are not being prosecuted as such, many believe, both in and out of the legal arena, that human trafficking is occurring elsewhere, and consequently, the funds and policies that would assist in combatting human trafficking are shifted elsewhere. Aside from the legal definitions, legal officials face many other unique challenges specific to human trafficking cases. Some of these challenges include: training, evolving law, jurisdiction, and targeted focus. Despite these challenges, police, federal agents, and prosecutors continue to pursue human trafficking investigations while combatting the problem at both the local and federal level. The following chapter will discuss not only the existing challenges, but also the successes based on case studies and personal attitudes of law enforcement officers. Additionally, this chapter will investigate the various training and investigative techniques that have proven to be beneficial for most, but which have begun to face new problems with the passage of new legislation.

Training

Sitting in a church pew, pen and paper in hand, we sit down to experience a human trafficking training seminar aimed specifically towards law enforcement officials in the city of St. Louis. We used our contacts with social service providers, many of whom coordinated the training activities, as well as our "criminologist" credentials to gain access to this training. Around the room, there are uniformed street level officers, federal agents, detectives, county sheriffs, as well as state and federal prosecutors. Additionally, there are social workers, medical doctors, and educators attending the training. Everyone seems to know everyone as we sit alone in our back pew, addressed by no one. We are definitely outsiders in this close-knit community. As the coffee is served and stale pastries are finally eaten, everyone takes a seat and the all-day training event begins. Immediately, as the first PowerPoint is uploaded, the realization becomes that this is not a training in the traditional sense. This will be a long day of presentations in which we will be talked to, audience interaction will be limited, and there will be virtually no hands-on activities that one would expect in the traditional training.

At this specific training, there are six presenters at the training: The Department of Labor, the Department of State, the FBI, Homeland Securities Investigations, the International Institute (a social service providing agency in St. Louis), and the District Attorney's Office. A representative from the Department of Labor begins the training by discussing the various types of labor visas offered, followed by the visa violations which are investigated. These violations include: padding and selling workers (requesting more visas than needed and then selling the overflow), overlapping petitions, failure to pay minimum wage and prevailing wage as required by the Department of Justice, charging of illegal fees, bait and switch (told to do one job but do another), and benching, which is keeping a pool of unpaid workers or not being paid for waiting to work. Each of these violations was discussed in Chapter Two. The law enforcement officials sitting in on the training are taught how to identify these visa violations, as well as what charges will be brought forth, and who will be handling the charging process, which is the State Department and Homeland Security. The speaker from the Department of State follows the representative from the Department of Labor and continues to discuss the various visa violations, emphasizing the need for law enforcement to recognize that those who purposely partake in document fraud are not to be treated as victims and should be prosecuted as criminals. Because most local level law enforcement officials are not trained in immigration enforcement, and therefore any immigration violation they face must be transferred to the federal authorities, the visa discussions are informative at most. From our observation, the only training that seemed to pique the interest of the local level law enforcement was the training conducted by the FBI.

There are two main divisions that handle human trafficking cases within the FBI: The Civil Rights Division and the Violent Crimes Division. In regards to identification, the speaker from the FBI admits that more cases of sex trafficking have been identified, although he is aware that labor trafficking is occurring. This seems to be the consensus amongst most law enforcement officials, specifically those officers in St. Louis and the metro-east communities (see Chapter Two). Beyond the general information, the speaker representing the FBI presents a cheat sheet for officers if they come into contact with a potential trafficking victim. This list of questions includes:

- What is your immigration status?
- How did you enter the United States?
- Do you have documents?
- Who is in control of your documents or travel?
- Do you have authorization to work in the United States?
- Were you told what to say to agents or officials when you arrived to the United States?
- Did you come for a specific job or purpose?
- Are you doing different work than you expected?

- Have you been threatened?
- What would happen if you left?
- Can you freely contact friends and family?
- Are you allowed to go to school?

Interestingly, this list of questions corresponds with many of the indicators of labor trafficking in St. Louis and the bi-state area, yet the speaker had already stated that the majority of victims identified in St. Louis are victims of sex trafficking. Additionally, the victim profile in St. Louis and the bi-state area tends to show that victims of sex trafficking are more likely to be US citizens whereas victims of labor trafficking tend to be foreign nationals. Yet, the list of "what law enforcement should ask" clearly has an emphasis on victims who are foreign nationals. It is this juxtaposition of "what we know" and "what we believe you should be doing" that leaves many law enforcement officials unhappy with the training they have received, or as some have suggested, the trainings are "pointless." This is just one example of the multiple trainings conducted by actors in the justice system that we attended over the course of three years. The dynamics of the other trainings, in both Illinois and Missouri were similar.

Local Level Law Enforcement Perceptions of Human Trafficking Trainings

After observing an example of a training local level law enforcement were required to sit through for an entire day, the authors felt it necessary to talk directly with law enforcement officials asking specific questions about their training and what they felt they learned from the experience. One officer believed that the only reason he was receiving the training was because the topic of human trafficking was a current trend:

> In law enforcement, you see ... trends and spikes. Like, 8 years ago, meth was the big popular go-to case. Now, it's heroin. And now, they're starting to try and push this human trafficking. Sometimes, when they have these hot

social topics, they push it a little bit farther than what I think the law's spirit is.

Other officers had similar opinions, simply called the topic of human trafficking "timely," or that the trainings were "just good timing."

Some officers felt that the training was simply for informational purposes only.

> [The basic content of the training is] identifying … what human trafficking is, what to look for, what resources are available, what the expectation of law enforcement is, what are the important collaboration between us and victims' services, and both the state and federal level on how a case will move forward. So, it is more of a familiarization with the district officers that would be coming into contact with these kinds of cases up front, so we are all kind of on the same page. It was more of awareness.

The third attitude that was identified with regards to officer perception of the training was that the training was important to their specific investigative roles, but may not be necessary for those who do not focus their efforts on trafficking cases. From one officer who specifically conducted online sting investigations:

> A lot of my training is intertwined as it relates to [human trafficking] … You may go to a sex crimes class which … it's not mainly specifically titled human trafficking or anything like that. Obviously, you know, they'll do refresher courses on the statistics or what we believe to be happening in our area, current crime trends, stuff like that …

The individuals who conduct the trainings had similar attitudes as to those who had been trained. According to one former US attorney, because she works with over a dozen municipalities, each with their own police departments, some officers might come across a human trafficking case but just might not know it. Therefore, the trainings are informational, providing indicators and phone numbers if human trafficking is suspected.

> The target audience for these will be local law enforcement: deputy sheriffs, highway patrol, state prosecutors ... and some social service agencies as well. [Our office is] just to say, 'here's an overview of what the main federal statutes are.' These are the considerations when you ... How to identify a federal case ... That is what these trainings are. What we consider a federal case, and what they need to present to us for us to pursue a federal case.

Another attorney described the trainings as simply "what is human trafficking, how do we recognize it, and what do we do when it looks like trafficking is happening."

All in all, the trainings are important for informational purposes only, yet with little hands-on experience or practice, the trainings become presentations. Many officers feel forced to participate and their interest gradually fades throughout the day. Other officers may already have an interest in human trafficking investigations, and already know the indicators and what to do when confronted with a suspected case of human trafficking. The trainings then become a "preaching to the choir" type scenario.

Do the authors believe that the trainings are irrelevant? Simply put, no, but they do need an overhaul. First of all, as indicated in a roundtable discussion at a human trafficking training in 2014, the trainers conducting the trainings need to be from the same group of people that are being trained. Although cross training is important in understanding one another's areas, such as social service provision and law enforcement (see Chapter Five), there is also the perception from those receiving the training that those who are conducting the trainings, for the most part, are far removed from the day to day activities of *local* level law enforcement. As previously stated, the trainers are federal agents and/or non-legal social service providers. Possibly, it would be more beneficial to conduct the training in a manner so that local level officers who are receiving the training hear another local level officer present on his/her experience when dealing with suspected trafficking cases. As such, the audience may be more inclined to believe that they too may confront human trafficking in their routine activities.

Secondly, there needs to be more interaction in the trainings. During a roundtable discussion with local law enforcement and agents from the FBI, officers indicated that if they are attending a training, they wanted it to actually be a training rather than presentation after presentation. They believed that the information given was important, but usually was left in a folder somewhere on their desks after the fact. If they had practice scenarios, instances in which they had to identify whether or not a person they had come into contact with was a perpetrator or potential victim, or take steps towards collecting evidence that would result in a successful prosecution; these and other activities would more likely resonate in their minds, more so than PowerPoint handouts. Those in law enforcement consistently indicated that interactive scenarios were what they wanted and needed in the trainings.

Overall, the training that law enforcement officials receive is necessary and the information provided is beneficial to an extent. Changes need to occur, but as long as officers are being provided with some sort of information, they are more likely to be able to identify potential trafficking cases. Unfortunately, even if they are fully aware of the law, how to identify potential victims, and what to do when trafficking is suspected, there are other obstacles that officers must overcome if we are to successfully prosecute offenders and protect victims in St. Louis and the bi-state area. The first of which is to consider the various perceptions of trafficking that officers hold in the community, and how these perceptions can impact investigations and prosecutions.

Officers' Perceptions of Trafficking in St. Louis and the Bi-State Area

The dichotomy between federal officers and local level officers is most prevalent when looking at the perceptions of and attitudes toward human trafficking in this community. The critical issue is law enforcement officials' viewpoints about whether or not trafficking is occurring in the St. Louis area. Because the majority of the cases that have been identified become federal cases, federal officers have a completely different attitude towards trafficking in the community when compared to the local level officers from the various municipalities. Other points of variance occur when looking at successful prosecutions and how trafficking cases are prosecuted. In the following pages, we will discuss how the handling and prosecution of human trafficking cases affects the overall perceptions of officers, and how these various perceptions affect the way human trafficking cases are investigated in St. Louis and the bi-state area.

In order to understand the perceptions of officers, there are various avenues that need to be investigated. The first of these is how trafficking cases are being identified and investigated. That in turn comes down to the types of trafficking that most believe are occurring in the area, as well as how and at what level the case will be prosecuted. These issues, tied together with an already existing framework regarding the prevalence of trafficking in the community, create an ambiguous assessment of human trafficking in St. Louis and the bi-state area. As already stated, this ambiguity begins at the investigative level.

Investigating Sex Trafficking Cases

Investigating human trafficking cases has the underlying problem, both for sex trafficking and labor trafficking, of the constant movement of the victims. In order to have a successful trafficking ring, traffickers must move victims from one hotel to another, or victims are transported from one labor site to another following the growing season. This mobility makes it difficult for investigators to not only track the trafficking activity, but also to maintain contact with a victim once he/she has been identified. As one officer stated:

> And the thing is that with trafficking, if ... If I'm trafficking you, and this is a common thing, and you're prosti-

tuting the different hotels, if I come and arrest you that night for prostitution, and him pimping, or I don't get him, I just get you, as soon as you make bond and you get released, the first thing he's doing is taking you to another state. So then there's no way for me to get in touch with you. There's no way for me to get you to go to court ... They move them people from out of here knowing, hey you're not gonna follow me to Virginia to find this lady to talk to her. And so, they're not dumb. They know, hey, as soon as we get into trouble here, we move either to a different state or somewhere far enough that you can't find us. Then, the first thing they do, the phone's gone, they got new pay phones, and then you've lost contact with your victims, so ... That's what makes it so incredibly hard to do anything with.

Therefore, once contact is made with a potential victim, keeping that victim or witness close for a successful prosecution has proven to be extremely problematic just based on the mobility of human trafficking. However, there are various techniques that legal officials use to identify potential victims, traffickers, and buyers.

At the local level, the identification of human trafficking situations generally occurs in one of two ways: online or during regular street patrols. Recognizably, these cases can also come to the attention of police through confidential source information or a lead in a missing child case, but at the local level the identification of perpetrators and victims is most likely to occur during an online sting operation or during a random traffic stop. In some rare instances, the victim will come forward to the police or social services, but this is relatively unlikely, and these cases generally have little evidence to provide for a successful prosecution. This is especially true when we look at the dichotomous relationship between human trafficking and domestic violence. As was previously discussed in Chapter Three, sex trafficking can occur in a combination of a number of other offenses, one of which is domestic violence. Advocates and federal agents are recognizing the relationship between domestic violence and sex trafficking, and are slowly working on training local level officers to identify trafficking indicators when confronted with a domestic violence case.

Unfortunately, at the local level, identifying domestic violence as a potential case of human trafficking has been met with some resistance. According to one local level officer:

> ... [G]oing back to something as simple as domestic [violence] ... a lot of times, the victim is still in love with the perpetrator. So, if I come to you, and I separate you in the heat of [the moment], usually what happens in the heat of the moment is, you'll say he's holding me against my will, he's making me do this, I hate him. But, then, once you cool down the next day ... you ask us to recant your statement because you didn't mean anything you said ... Nowadays, you need proof beyond proof to win in court. It's not the good ol' days of he, he said that ... a cop said he said that, the victim said he said that ... it doesn't work that way, unfortunately.

This resistance to the relationship between domestic violence and human trafficking not only creates a dilemma of recanting statements with no evidence, but in some instances, a report will never be filed by the local level police. According to a legal advocate:

> ... [S]everal of our clients have been [or] are domestic violence survivors, but there was also trafficking involved in their cases. But, what we see sometimes is that law enforcement will not have made a record of them calling the police ... I think law enforcement gets so many calls for domestic violence that they get desensitized to it. And so they've just stopped making reports of it.

In those cases in which the victim comes forward for assistance, specifically domestic violence cases, there is a level of resistance on the level of local police to identify a relationship to trafficking, and unfortunately in some cases, even report the instance. Thus, when looking at investigative strategies, we are aware that victims may come forward to the police, but these cases may not be regarded as trafficking cases. Rather, the cases that are predominantly identified as human trafficking are those cases that have been identified by local level officers either through proactive online investigations or routine street patrol.

Using the Internet as an investigative tool has proven to be very successful in identifying human trafficking situations, specifically in cases of sex trafficking. By necessity, traffickers need to post an advertisement for the victim in order to find the potential buyers. For officers, as well as the general public, the Internet provides an uncomplicated means to identify what could potentially be a sex trafficking situation. In terms of investigating human trafficking though the Internet, local level officers generally create a fake profile, and in collaboration with federal officers, hope to generate enough evidence to charge the potential buyers. For example, one local level officer described the process as the following: "We set up a house, secret service, US Attorney, sheriff's department, state police, and we just went online and said, here is my daughter. She's seven. If you want to have sex with her, here's the price, get a hold of me. And then all day, all we do is try to work the deal." That is the general investigative strategy to identify potential buyers, and has proven to be a successful tool in investigation and prosecution. Unfortunately, as will be discussed later in the chapter, using the Internet as a tool of investigation is now being met with new obstacles as laws are created against online advertising.

Using the Internet is the more common method of trafficking investigation, but local level officers are also aware that trafficking can also be identified in routine investigations. During a routine traffic stop, it is likely that the officer could come into contact with the victim(s) and/or trafficker(s). Again, as with all other investigative techniques, the officer needs to look beyond the surface and away from the ordinary to determine if a simple speeding violation could be connected to human trafficking. For example:

> ... [A] young male pimp ... was going from Illinois down to Memphis, and he had two girls with him; they were sisters. One sister had worked for him as a prostitute already in Illinois. The younger sister had not. It was not the younger sister's intention to be involved ... I think the de-

fendant had a different idea! But, they were headed down
to Memphis, and I believe that he would have done whatever he could to try to persuade them to stay with him for
a long time. He got caught, and that was a happenstance
case. [It was a] high-speed chase on the 55, on a traffic
stop and it kind of just, 'Oh, what are you three doing together?' Oh, it's plausible they're just going on a road
trip ... Then [the officers] do a little bit of checking. 'Oh,
there's a missing person's report for the girls. I guess
you're not just going on a road trip!'

Although it does take extra initiative on the part of the officer to
look beyond the surface of a routine traffic stop, the majority of
local level officers interviewed for this project were fully aware of
the possibility of coming into contact with a potential trafficker
and/or victim. As one officer clearly stated, "the traffickers have to
take people in transit to get to and from, so how do they get stopped
in transit? Some traffic violation!" Therefore, in order to come into
first contact with a trafficker and/or victim, traffic stops seem to be
more beneficial. On the buyer side, the Internet has proven to be
more useful in the creation of fake ads and catching the potential
buyers, who are charged with sex trafficking (see Chapter Three).

Online Challenges for Law Enforcement

Although the Internet has been found to be a useful tool in investigation, law enforcement now faces new obstacles in investigating human trafficking. The Internet has proven to be incredibly
useful for traffickers because it is anonymous, websites can be en-
crypted, websites can be removed, and traffickers can advertise victims for sale for free on a number of public sites. Traffickers are
also able to offer jobs to potential victims of labor trafficking. Because we know more about the strategies of the traffickers than we
do of the traffickers themselves, legislators and advocates have
fought to have these advertisements removed and criminalized. Because of those efforts, new laws are being passed that does exactly
that: criminalizing sex for sale ads found on the Internet.

On May 20, 2014, the US House of Representatives overwhelmingly passed the Stop Advertising Victims of Exploitation (SAVE) Act, which was authored by Congresswoman Ann Wagner from the 2nd District of Missouri. In short the SAVE Act criminalizes the advertising of minors for sex on websites such as Craigslist and Backpage. The SAVE Act "amends Section 1591 of the Federal Criminal Code, inserting 'advertises' into the list of conduct that comprise the crime of federal sex trafficking" (http:// wagner.house.gov/notforsale, accessed June 2014). If found guilty, any person advertising a minor under the age of 14 will be sentenced to a minimum of 15 years.

In addition to punishing the person advertising sex for sale, the Save Act also "requires a person to have knowingly benefitted financially or otherwise from the sale of such advertising to be punished" (H.R. 4225, SAVE Act, 2014). In other words, sponsoring sites, such as google.com, backpage.com, or craigslist.com, can also be punished under the Act if the site providers are aware of the possibility that a child may have been advertised in a sex for sale advertisement, but chose to not report the site or have the advertisement removed. This provision recognizes those sponsor sites that make money off of a sex trafficking enterprise simply by turning away from a potential trafficking situation. This is the case even if the provider is aware without certainty that the advertisement is sex trafficking.

On paper, and through media and political spin, this law sounds as if it is the first step of many in the eradication of human trafficking in the United States. Truly, it seems, there is no better way to stop trafficking than by blocking the means traffickers use to advertise their victims. However, the SAVE Act is introducing new problems as police attempt to combat trafficking. The main problem that is being identified by those interviewed in this project is that the SAVE Act not only blocks an advertising avenue for human traffickers, specifically those trafficking for purposes of sexual exploitation, but it also unintentionally blocks an integral tool in investigative techniques for law enforcement. First of all, some officers felt that this legislation would do nothing more than move the advertising from one website to the next. As one officer explained: "The thing with that [blocking activities on a website] is if you block it on one website, the next website is fine." He continued to compare the blocking of advertising sites to the previous legislative efforts of blocking Internet activity:

"It's like ... Napster back in the day. Well, here's Napster; everybody is downloading music, [and] that's illegal. Well, there's 42 other 'Napster' sites that aren't illegal ... They close one site down, and then there's ten others ... It doesn't matter where it's at. The people that are perverts, they're gonna know [where to go]."

In our own previous research (See Heil and Nichols, 2014), we theoretically argued that these legislative efforts will just displace the activities of traffickers, as just indicated, from one website to the next. However, some of those interviewed felt that this new legislation did deserve some merit. For example, one officer began discussing the legislation by looking at it as a tool to cut off traffickers at their source: " ... In one respect ... we use [the Internet] as a tool to proactively get these people. But I think overall, if it was outlawed, then you would definitely ... I think it would be better for it to be outlawed, because if it is eradicated, you will be cutting it off at its [source]." When followed up with a clarification question regarding eradication, he demonstrated a concern for displacement: "I think [the trafficking activities] would either probably go somewhere else, or they would change the way the wording is on it and redirect you to maybe a different website potentially or a server that is not in this country but would somehow ultimately facilitate the transaction ..." This officer clearly agreed that steps need to be taken to deter potential traffickers, and this deterrence might simply be by blocking websites. However, blocking and eradication are two different things, and we may simply be redirecting the activity to other websites causing it to be more difficult to identify and protect potential victims.

One officer interviewed explained how he attempted to uncover some of the hidden activity via new websites by retrieving information from junior high students. According to him, there was a hot new social media site being used by younger generations. He had never heard of this site, but decided to go ahead and investigate what type of information was easily accessible to these children, as well as potential traffickers. According to the officer: "I just created a fake profile one day at the office just to see kinda what would happen, and I'm like, 'Who's got pics? [I] love young kids.' My screen filled up so fast I had to shut it down because I had so many people sending me requests for their files." As more and more of these websites are created, it becomes more difficult for law enforcement officials to utilize the tool. If we continue to block one source of investigation, a new one will be developed and as clearly stated by one officer, "there's not enough cops in the world to track all that down."

Website activity moving from one site to another is just one problem that law enforcement officials are facing when using the Internet as a tool in investigation. A very new problem is having an undercover sting operation online taken down by online service providers before any investigations can occur. In other words, online service providers are blocking what they believe to be a potential advertisement sexually exploiting a child, when in reality, it is a fake advertisement used to draw out the buyer. As one officer explained to me, "In some recent undercover schemes we've done, when we're doing the undercover part of it, they've even turned us in to the National Center of Missing and Exploited Children. So some of the electronic service providers are doing their job, but at the same time, we can't catch the bad guys ..." Because we are in the early stages of working with the new law, coupled with the already existing surveillance policies, law enforcement officials are finding that the one tool of investigation that had been used primarily in the identification of victims is now being blocked both by the online service providers and by innovative legal maneuvers created by policymakers.

In addition to the issues associated with the actual websites stems the problem of how the information online is retrieved. Recently, questions regarding the role of agencies such as the National Center of Missing and Exploited Children (NCMEC) and their capabilities of searching online sites without a warrant has come to the attention of the US Courts. In *United States of America v. David Keith*

(2013), in which Keith was "charged with distribution of child pornography ... and possession and accessing child pornography...," the federal court ruled that "[i]n examining the contents of the emailed image file from the defendant's computer that was uploaded to its CyberTipline server, NCMEC was acting as an agent of federal law enforcement, and the Fourth Amendment applied ... Accordingly, NCMEC's examination of the contents of that emailed image file violated the Fourth Amendment because it was not authorized by a duly issued warrant" (2013). In other words, agencies working as the middle man, such as NCMEC, are now considered agents of the state, and therefore, any information retrieved online is considered a legal search. Without a warrant, that information could be deemed inadmissible if the Court feels the search violated the defendant's Fourth Amendment right. As one local officer explained with regards to the Court's ruling, " ... I understand the point of the ruling, but ... it's definitely new ground I guess I should say as far as these organizations to be careful to how much they inject themselves into the situation before they become an agent of the state for law enforcement." Thus, not only do local level police have to be concerned with their own online initiatives being blocked, but also if they receive any sort of tip, they must question whether or not the information received from the tip falls under the fruit of the poison tree doctrine in that the information was obtained illegally and therefore considered inadmissible.

As new laws are created in an effort to protect potential victims of sex trafficking, law enforcement officials are finding that their job of identifying the offenders, both buyers and traffickers, is becoming more difficult as obstacles to online investigations are being created. They are now being forced to seek out new avenues of advertising to investigate, or they must maneuver through online service providers and try to apprehend the offender before the sting operation is shut down. Lastly, they must be weary of the legality of the information they receive from any online tip group. Certainly, this is not just an issue for law enforcement officials in St. Louis and the bi-state area as these laws affect law enforcement officials throughout the United States. However, given that each officer interviewed for this project openly expressed an opinion and concern regarding the direction of legislation with regard to online activities, this issue is of extreme importance for the officers in this community as they question their own investigative techniques and the legality of these techniques. As one officer so aptly stated, "I don't know if I agree with it, but obviously, [we've] got to be [more] cautious."

Although there are online challenges when conducting human trafficking investigations, those challenges are intimately tied to sex trafficking investigations. What has been incredibly absent from the discussion of investigative strategies is how to investigate a potential labor trafficking case.

Investigating Labor Trafficking Cases

As was discussed in Chapter Two, it is a common perception in St. Louis and the bi-state area that labor trafficking is occurring, and there is awareness that it is occurring in agricultural fields, factories, restaurants, beauty salons, and construction work. However, the number of labor trafficking cases that have been investigated as such are few and far between. This is because, for the most part, labor trafficking cases are much more difficult to investigate than sex trafficking cases. According to a former federal prosecutor:

> We know that there is a lot of labor trafficking probably here. We have not prosecuted as many labor trafficking cases. I'm not exactly sure why. That's one of the things that I'm trying to figure out and see if it's an investigative issue, or if it's somehow easier to hide. There's certainly not as much advertising when you're trafficking someone for labor. Once you have them, they often keep them and keep them hidden.

Unfortunately, for the victims of labor trafficking, because this victimization is so hidden and victims are not repeatedly sold, the investigative tools of law enforcement are limited.

That is not to say that investigations are not occurring, but the investigations of labor trafficking are both geographically and federally limited. The majority of local-level law enforcement interviewed for this project admitted to not investigating labor trafficking cases. Specifically officers in St. Louis and the surrounding communities recognized there is the potential of labor trafficking occurring in the metro-east region, but it is not something they have really considered. Not a single officer from St. Louis or the metro-east believed they had come into contact with a labor trafficking situation. As one officer responded when asked if he had ever heard of labor trafficking cases in the St. Louis and metro-east region, his response was, "I'm not aware of anything. That's something definitely to be mindful of. I mean it could be ... underneath the surface, but you are not really focused on somebody working illegally versus somebody being sexually exploited." Another officer believed that labor trafficking was not something that was occurring in St. Louis and the metro-east, "but it's more in the larger states that it's happening." Thus, in St. Louis and the metro-east communities, labor trafficking was not viewed as a real problem, especially by local-level officers.

Although local-level officers do not believe they have not come into contact with labor trafficking situations, some local officers are working on building awareness campaigns with the insular ethnic communities in the area. Unfortunately, even outreach to these communities can be met with obstacles. According to one detective, "We just did an awareness thing and talked with the Hispanic leadership group ... The hard thing is you've got a very diverse group of people so naturally they don't trust the police depending on what country they're from ... Then you've got immigration status issues which keeps people from coming forward." Despite these obstacles, the detective felt hopeful that he would be able to work with some of the communities and identify more potential labor trafficking cases: "We're hopin' that we can get ... these different communities. Whether it's the Hispanic, the Bosnian community, which is big here ... the Asian community.... get down to work since [labor trafficking is] growing out here." Therefore, there is a shift in awareness with regards to the occurrence of labor trafficking in St. Louis and the surrounding communities, and some officers are taking proactive measures to reach out to potential victims.

At the federal level, law enforcement officers were more aware of the possibility of labor trafficking occurring in St. Louis and the metro-east communities. According to one FBI agent, there had not been many reports on forced labor, but "we know it's going on." However, it was also acknowledged that many of the cases remained unreported because of an immigration issue. As was stated earlier, the majority of those identified in labor trafficking situations tend to be foreign nationals. Therefore, there is the underlying issue of deportation and victims are reluctant to talk when identified by law enforcement. In addition to the fear of deportation, there is a challenge within the immigrant communities because "the traffickers are of the same ethnicity." As one officer reported, "[t]hey definitely prey on their own."

In these sensitive cases, law enforcement officials must go beyond traditional investigative techniques in order to obtain the whole story from the potential victim. According to one interviewee who observed a case conducted by an Immigration and Customs Enforcement (ICE) agent:

> There were a couple of guys who were working for ... a roofing company, and they were ... being severely maltreated. And they were undocumented. And the ICE agent kept [saying], 'Look, I'm not going to—I just want you to tell me the truth and tell me what was going on.' And they weren't comfortable. And then [the ICE agent] said, 'Would you like me to let you call your mother in Mexico?' And so the guy calls his mother, and his mother says, 'Tell him the truth of what's happened to you.' And so he told the truth. And it was clearly a labor trafficking situation. But this was an ICE agent who ... really knew that this guy was being exploited and [he was] trying to find a way to get him to feel secure enough.

In addition to using creative investigative techniques to alleviate reluctance, law enforcement officials are likely to collaborate with an immigration attorney to help put the potential victim at ease. This is because the potential victim is aware that the conversation between him or her and the attorney is confidential, and the immigration attorney can patiently listen as the story develops. The potential victim also feels more comfortable with a person that will advocate for him and work with law enforcement on any immigration issues.

Clearly sex trafficking cases deal with sensitive issues, but because in the bi-state area the majority of labor trafficking victims that have been identified as foreign nationals, labor trafficking cases force officers to pursue investigations through layers of immigration status, fear of deportation, fear of community, language barriers, and migration patterns. Because of this, specific training is being conducted in those areas that are most likely to come into contact with a potential victim of labor trafficking. In other words, trainings are not only being conducted specifically for federal law enforcement agents, but also local level officers in rural communities.

In rural communities, it has been difficult to get local level police committed to the local anti-trafficking effort. This could be because of political reasons, for as one local advocate stated, " ... I think it was political because they thought with the farmers in the area ... [it was better for the police to stay out of any sort of conflict]." However, after constant pressure at the local advocacy level, as well as networking throughout the state, at the time of this writing, every sheriff in that state eventually received training with an emphasis on labor trafficking in the rural areas. Unfortunately, with all of the training that is being provided for law enforcement and advocates alike, identification and investigation of labor trafficking still has the overwhelming obstacle of gaining the trust and cooperation of the victims themselves. One member of a legal outreach team clearly stated, as discussed fully in Chapter Two, "it is very tough [to identify], because they won't talk. 'I just don't want to get in trouble. I don't have water, but I don't want to say anything ...'" In other words, as previously stated, and had been stated by many of our interviewees, "[sex trafficking is] more noticeable. You've got clients, you've got all that interaction, and with labor trafficking it just may be a crew leader and that one person." Therefore, although attempts are being made to identify labor trafficking in the bi-state area, as well as to punish the offenders and protect the victims, significant barriers still exist. Mainly, there is very little public interaction and the victims are in a constant state of fear, consequently, local level officers are fighting an uphill battle while attempting to investigate labor trafficking. Whether it is labor trafficking or sex trafficking, the majority of the cases in the bi-state area are treated as federal cases. In the following section, it will be discussed how these cases become federal cases, and why a federal case is preferred to all parties involved.

From State Level to Federal Level

At the early stages of a potential human trafficking case, the first responders are generally local level police. They may be called in for a domestic violence situation, a labor violation, or a sexual assault. Generally, the process of the case being brought to the attention of the police is as follows:

> The first person that gets contacted with that would be our dispatchers; you know 911 would of course take the call. It's fed into a computerated dispatching system that dispatches it to a district officer, patrol officer that would be first contact with the victim. That officer would establish the communication, what happened. And it, by procedure, we would, that officer would contact, if it is a sex crimes related case, he would contact our office, sex crimes. If it is a labor related case, they would immediately contact the district detective bureau. There is actually in each of the 9 districts in St. Louis, they have a detective bureau investigation group of detectives that work out of that. They would contact them and intelligence. And that's the initial start-up, and then the investigation would begin.

After the initial investigation, if the local level officer suspects human trafficking, the protocol is to call the FBI. At this point the investigation can go back and forth between state level and federal level. For example, there may state level charges available for the offender or the charges may not meet the level of federal charges. This once again comes back to the legal definitions of human trafficking. Federally, human trafficking must involve some form of force, fraud, or coercion, unless it is a commercial sex act involving a minor. Therefore, if there is not enough evidence that meets that criteria, the case may be pushed back to the state level. State laws, however, may not require that element, and therefore the case can still be tried as a human trafficking case at the state level. For example, in Missouri, the law has been re-written and has expanded the element of means to not only include force, fraud or coercion, but also to include, but not limited to the following: "force, abduction, coercion, fraud, deception, blackmail, or causing or threatening to cause financial harm" (State of Missouri, House Bill No. 214). Because Missouri has an expanded definition of the means element, many of the cases that do not meet the federal definition of human trafficking and cannot be charged as such may still be able to be charged as a human trafficking case at the state level.

In the relationship between federal and state level prosecutions, most cases that have the evidence to meet the legal definition of human trafficking will more likely be prosecuted at the federal level. This is not necessarily a bad thing. In fact, as one officer stated, " ... we always want to go to a federal charge. It's a lot nicer sitting in a federal prison than a state penitentiary or city jail over here." According to a federal prosecutor, "[m]ost state and federal law enforcement officers are very eager to have their cases prosecuted federally—they consider that a good thing!" Once the case goes to the federal level, the local level police work on their own continuing cases, and the cycle continues as the next case is investigated. This relationship is working well in the bi-state area, but once the case reaches that level of prosecution, whether it be a state prosecution or federal prosecution, there are additional challenges for the prosecutor before there can be a successful prosecution.

Challenges for Prosecution

As was already discussed, one of the greatest challenges for the prosecution is the evidentiary burden. As the case moves through the investigative process, most of the initial evidence is going to be derived through victim or trafficker testimony. As one prosecutor explained:

> These cases come in one of two ways. We've got potential traffickers or we've got potential victims. It's very rare that anyone is going to be completely honest about what's going on, at first. So from a legal standpoint it can become very difficult because we almost have to assume that most victims are going to lie to us at first, because they're scared, or they're here illegally and they've been told they're going to be deported, or something is going to happen to their family members somewhere else, or locally, or they think they're going to be prosecuted as a co-conspirator. So there is all kinds of motivations for them to lie ... I always assume that I've not gotten the full story, because the agents have not gotten the full story, when they first encounter a victim, or they first encounter a trafficker, and then, it becomes a matter of what else can we use to corroborate what our victim is saying. Knowing also that time is of the essence because if someone is out there we don't have the luxury of maybe of another type of case ...

Therefore, the first challenge for prosecutors is to get the whole story. As this prosecutor indicated, that is going to be rare, so other evidence must be collected in order corroborate the force, fraud, or coercion, and collecting this evidence is going to take time. Unfortunately, as one police officer highlighted, "it may take a year to get all the information ... and in that process, you can lose [the victim]." Therefore, the first challenge is identifying a victim with a consistent story who will remain and participate throughout the investigative process and the prosecution.

Unfortunately, the ideal victim does not exist. Victims will change their story from the story provided at the initial identification, as s/he will be traumatized or may otherwise be reluctant to implicate the trafficker in a crime. S/he can't sort out all of the events that have occurred, or s/he is afraid of what will happen if s/he tells the truth. Therefore, the story changes or s/he lies. This in turn becomes a tool for the defense. According to a federal prosecutor, "if I have to put somebody on the stand who's made a prior inconsistent statement, then that makes them ripe for fertile cross examination. [A defense attorney can legitimately ask] 'well, you had a chance to tell your story, and you lied didn't you?'" If the jury believes that because of a changing story, the truth is not beyond a reasonable doubt, the prosecutor is unlikely to have a successful case.

Additionally, many of the victims that testify are not viewed as victims worthy of sympathy, which is an additional challenge for prosecutors. Many of the victims that testify against their traffickers can also be legally identified as criminals, for they may have been forced into prostitution, drug use, or illegal immigration. Not only will the defense attorney highlight the inconsistencies in the story, but he may also look at the moral credibility of the victim. As one officer explained:

> The first thing [the defense attorney] is gonna do is say, well, she's a prostitute, she's got five drug convictions ... Unfortunately, instead of the bad guy being put on the stand, the victims ... always get picked [as] the ones that get targeted and [are told] you're not credible, you're not credible ... You can't convict this; there's no proof. And that's what [the prosecutors] tell you, there's no proof.

With any type of case, the prosecutor is not going to take a case that he/she cannot win. Unfortunately, politics still come into play when dealing with prosecutors, and they do not want cases that will go against their record. So those cases that eventually do make it to prosecution must involve a credible victim that the jury will likely have sympathy for, and these victims, especially in human trafficking cases, are rare. As stated, the victims that are being identified are socially viewed as prostitutes, drug users, or "illegal aliens." This is an image obstacle that, for prosecutors trying to influence a jury, is difficult to overcome. Because of the evidentiary and victim issues, many times prosecutors will charge the defendant with a charge that will more likely "stick." Traffickers are being charged with promoting prostitution, visa fraud, wage per hour violations, etc., each of which have penalties ranging from two to sixty years plus fines depending on the degree or class of the felony. Trafficking may even be reduced to a misdemeanor charge, such as pimping or pandering.

Another issue confronted by prosecutors is keeping witnesses and potential victims available throughout the entire process, from investigation through prosecution. Many cases may first be identified as a potential trafficking case, but somehow get stopped or lost, possibly because of a victim disappearing or recanting the statement, because of lack of evidence, or because the victim is not identified accordingly (e.g., prostitute rather than trafficking victim). This has been referred by some of those interviewed as the leaky pipeline. As one officer explained, "So, you have coming into the pipe line, you have a number of people that you [suspect] as trafficking victims, and then at the end, you have the ones that actually get characterized as a trafficking victim. But then, [there is] some kind of fall out ... for various reasons." Those interviewed for this project indicated that the majority of those cases that are lost or do not make it to prosecution as a human trafficking are because of the misidentification. According to a local officer:

> We are at 80-something rapes just here in St. Louis alone. A lot of those sometimes involve prostitutes, and there may even be some human trafficking involved in those cases. But, you see where they stop is at the state of sexual assault or forcible rape, or whatever the charge is on the sex side of it. It doesn't elevate to that human trafficking if that's not what we're ... looking at ...

That attitude seems to be the consensus amongst the majority of the officers interviewed for this project. Human trafficking is not being seen for what it is, it is not being looked for, and for one very honest officer interviewed for this project, "[human trafficking law] is not enforced or looked at just because of the way ... those cases are shaped out." In other words, because of the evidentiary burden, the lack of "credible" witnesses, and the misidentification, specifically at the local level, human trafficking cases are incredibly challenging to the prosecution in establishing a successful case.

Chapter Summary

Throughout St. Louis and the bi-state area, local and federal level law enforcement officials face unique challenges when dealing with human trafficking cases. Given these unique challenges, trainings are being conducted to teach officers the various victim indicators, as well as what to do when confronting a potential victim, trafficker, or buyer. Unfortunately, the trainings are met with some resistance, especially at the level of local law enforcement, many of who believe the trainings are nothing more than feeding a social and media-hyped trend. Other officers claimed to already have knowledge of human trafficking based on their specific area of enforcement, and found the trainings to be nothing more than informational. Given that, we argue that the trainings need to become more meaningful, providing not only information, but hands-on practice. Additionally, the trainings need to be conducted by the same pool of individuals who are being trained (i.e., local level officers training local level officers).

Beyond the trainings, officers face a distinct challenge when investigating trafficking cases. Given the underlying crimes that may be occurring concurrently with the trafficking, such as immigration issues, domestic violence, or rape, officers may not look beyond the surface and will only identify the crime providing the most evidence. Therefore, officers investigate human trafficking, specifically sex trafficking, by conducting online sting operations or by looking for indicators during routine traffic stops. Online investigations have proven to be more beneficial when targeting buyers while protecting victims, but this investigative strategy is slowly being blocked as new legislation is being passed regarding the illegal advertising of sex for sale online.

Labor trafficking investigations, on the other hand, are rarely conducted, especially in St. Louis and the metro-east. Any labor trafficking cases that may be viewed as such are usually moved through the prosecutorial process as visa violation charges for the potential trafficker or immigration violation charges for the potential victim. Even in the instances of visa or immigration violations, officers must create ingenious techniques to earn the trust of the potential victim or witness, because there is the underlying fear of deportation that generally exists with labor trafficking cases.

Once a human trafficking case has been investigated and there is enough evidence to prosecute, prosecutors must overcome obstacles such as victims becoming unavailable; witnesses not being credible because of an inherent criminal history associated with human trafficking (e.g., undocumented immigrants, prostitution, or drug use); or not having enough evidence to prosecute the case as a human trafficking case. In those instances when human trafficking is prosecuted as another offense, such as rape or domestic violence, the prevalence of human trafficking in St. Louis and the bi-state area becomes questionable. If the numbers are unavailable, local level officers will come to believe that it is not occurring in their backyard, and are less likely to look for the general indicators.

Overall, in St. Louis and the bi-state area, measures are being taken to improve the investigation and prosecution of human trafficking. However, there is still much work that needs to be done. Trainings need to be reformatted. Labor trafficking cases need to be identified as such, and sex trafficking cases need to be identified in conjunction with other crimes that may be co-occurring. Officers and prosecutors need the necessary time and resources to investigate and prosecute human trafficking cases successfully. Despite the existing challenges, and even under skewed numbers of actual cases, officers and prosecutors are aware of the occurrence of human trafficking in St. Louis and the bi-state area, and are using what resources they have to ultimately protect victims and punish offenders.

Chapter 5

Community Responses to Trafficking: Education, Training, Outreach and Collaboration

Beyond the legal arena in which traffickers are being identified and prosecuted exists the various groups that provide education and training to law enforcement, so that they are able to *properly* identify and prosecute traffickers. These social service providing groups, many of which are not-for-profit, not only educate and train law enforcement officials, but also those members of the community who are most likely to come into contact with potential victims of human trafficking. The relationship between social service providers and law enforcement can sometimes be stressed because of conflicting ideas and goals (e.g., victim support vs. victim testimony), yet each agency must overcome these obstacles so that they are able to work with one another, as well as with members of the community. The collaboration between law enforcement, social service providers, and the community is crucial in properly identifying and protecting victims, while at the same time, punishing the offenders, and that collaboration can only exist through education, training, and outreach initiatives.

Chapter Five examines community-based responses to human trafficking. Specifically, we explore the work of organizations that provide education, awareness, and training to the public and other professionals about human trafficking, as well as collaboration between these organizations in their anti-trafficking efforts. Such groups are vital in the efforts towards identifying and responding to both labor and sex trafficking victimization. Significant progress in various aspects of anti-trafficking efforts, as well as identification of key areas that presented challenges in the St. Louis bi-state area, are depicted throughout this chapter. The aim is to offer insights into the anti-trafficking efforts of the study site, and to provide information that may assist other sites with similar contextual dynamics in developing or revising their own anti-trafficking efforts. Community awareness, outreach, collaboration, and training were all described as successful avenues of progress. Yet gaps were identified within these areas that needed to be addressed. The anti-trafficking responses found to be successful, as well as responses that presented challenges or were lacking, are examined in detail in the following sections.

Efforts toward Identification

Identification is important in addressing human trafficking. Social services and the justice system largely depend on survivors to come forward to seek assistance and to report victimization, as trafficking is known to be challenging to identify (Nichols & Heil, 2014). Yet, as indicated in Chapter One, survivors may not seek out assistance from social services or law enforcement for a variety of different reasons. Consequently, an emphasis of the anti-trafficking movement, fuelled by provisions included in the TVPA, highlights identification of human trafficking by ordinary citizens, law enforcement, social service providers, and front line workers through education, training, and community awareness programs, as well as direct outreach to survivors. These endeavors aim to increase identification of victims, resulting in increased prosecution of traffickers and service provision to survivors.

Community Awareness

Most of the major anti-trafficking organizations in the St. Louis bi-state area offer some form of community education and awareness including the Rescue and Restore Coalitions of St. Louis and Southwestern Illinois, The International Institute, The Covering House, Magdalene House, Youth in Need, The Dignity Network, The Exchange Initiative, and others. Respondents in this study consistently cited community awareness of sex trafficking as a major strength of anti-trafficking responses in the St. Louis Metro area. For example, one social service provider stated:

> I think St. Louis, in general, is doing a great job of making people aware of it. It seems like depending on what field you go into, everybody kind of has a basic knowledge of it, or they're starting to get a basic knowledge of it. They're hearing the word, they're able to put trafficking and exploitation together, they're starting to make some of those connections. So … you're not just seeing small little pockets of it, it's kind of starting to spread out and that awareness piece is kind of growing a lot.

Similarly, when asked about "what worked" in St. Louis, another social service provider gave a response typical of most respondents, "What's working is awareness. Awareness is growing through Rescue & Restore, through The Covering House, through Magdalene House, other agencies and organizations too." The "spreading out" and expansion of awareness was largely attributed to community education and training of professionals. Presentations providing education on the basic dynamics of sex trafficking or commercial sexual exploitation were given at religious organizations, K–12 schools, local community colleges and universities, and other community organizations. Awareness and education presentations included, but were not limited to: basic explanations of what sex trafficking is, warning signs of a sex trafficking situation, how someone might become a sex trafficking victim, and how to respond to a potential sex trafficking situation through the national hotline.

Presentations to community members related to labor trafficking were much more limited compared to presentations about sex trafficking, likely because relatively fewer social service organizations in St. Louis specifically dealt with labor trafficking victims. This was a gap recognized as an area in need of further development by various members of the anti-trafficking community. The International Institute and Rescue and Restore Coalitions were the organizations largely involved in providing education about labor trafficking (see also Chapter Two), whereas these organizations plus The Covering House, Magdalene House, Youth in Need, and others additionally provided community presentations about sex trafficking. Labor trafficking presentations generally involved defining labor trafficking and the forms it may take, red flag indicators of labor trafficking, and how to respond to a suspected labor trafficking situation.

In addition to community presentations, informational handouts about sex and labor trafficking were provided at local festivals and community events through the Rescue and Restore coalitions. Further, through social media, information about labor and sex trafficking were also disseminated to the larger community. Importantly, such awareness efforts were aimed at addressing identification of trafficking with the idea that ordinary citizens could provide tips and report suspicious activities. Such efforts have not yet been evaluated, as they are relatively new. Regardless, community awareness holds additional value.

Aside from identification from citizen-offered tips, community awareness is important for public and political support of governmental and private resources and funding available to survivors of human trafficking. For example, when the battered women's movement garnered public and political support, funding streams increased, allowing for the development of shelters, hotlines, and other important resources. Without public and political support, widespread availability of resources and increased accountability of abusers would not have occurred (Nichols, 2014). Likewise, public and political support is necessary for the development and provision of resources for sex and labor trafficking survivors as well. The unquestionable need for such services is highlighted in Chapter Six.

Training for Professionals and Front-Line Workers

Another key component of education and awareness in the St. Louis bi-state area, aside from presentations for members of the general community, involved the education and training of professionals likely to come into contact with trafficked people. This included service providers, healthcare providers, and law enforcement (law enforcement training is described in Chapter Four). For example, the staff of Birthright received training, with the idea that trafficked women or girls may seek assistance related to an unplanned pregnancy. Seminary students and other faith-based ministries received training with the idea that a trafficked person may contact them for help or advice. Child services staff, hospital staff working in OBGYN, professionals who work with the homeless, staff who administrate the WIC program, interpreters, law enforcement, domestic violence victim advocates and service providers, and service providers for sexual assault victims also received training through Rescue and Restore coalitions in the bi-state area, as they had been identified as among those most likely to come into contact with a trafficked person. The director of Rescue and Restore St. Louis described this training:

> ... we also train social service providers, law enforcement, and healthcare professionals. And they may or may not have a background in the human trafficking industry, but they will have some knowledge of victim services and that kind of a thing. So, we train them how to recognize it in their setting. So, it's more specific than what we would give to the general community. So, what are the red flags that they will see in their job? What are the indicators that they will see? And then, we encourage them to set up a protocol.

The Rescue and Restore coalitions of St. Louis and Southwestern Illinois appeared to be the groups most involved in implementing training for various professionals, although other organizations participated in various trainings as well, such as the Covering House and the International Institute. The coalition training was conducted at times in partnership with the FBI victim specialist based in St. Louis, Legal Services of Eastern MO, the Exchange Initiative, and the International Institute, among others. The Covering House, the St. Louis County Police Department, and the St. Louis City Police Department also partnered in training. Training for frontline workers typically included the same information as the community presentations; training then addressed specific dynamics each group may distinctly encounter based upon their positions.

As one example of professional-specific training, in circumstances in which healthcare providers encounter patients with recurring STDs and signs of mental and physical abuse, coupled with
an office visit where someone else accompanies the patient, controls the conversation, and must be present, training indicates this
may be a warning sign of sex trafficking (Rescue and Restore,
2014). Illness typically resulting from unsanitary living conditions
or signs of limited healthcare, coupled with an individual possessing the patient's documents, and who controls the conversation
and insists on serving as an interpreter, may be a sign of labor or
sex trafficking (Rescue and Restore, 2014). All trainings conclude
with a suggestion to call the National Human Trafficking Resource
Center (NHTRC), to report and connect with local resources to
coordinate and address the potential problem.

As another example of professional-specific training, several organizations were involved in training hotel staff. As discussed in
Chapter Three, hotels are common venues for sex trafficking. Consequently, hotel staff are some of the most likely potential front-
line identifiers of sex trafficking. At least two organizations in St.
Louis worked with ECPAT, an international anti-trafficking organization which created a Code of Conduct for travel and tourism.
This Code works to prevent and identify sex trafficking, in part by
training hotel staff. The director of the Exchange Initiative stated:

> We support the Child Protection Code of Conduct for
> travel and tourism…. when we go to hotels, they're usu-
> ally shocked. Several hotels have trained and we're very
> pleased—if you don't sign the code at least you're bring-
> ing awareness. So in the past five years I have seen very
> good progress in the training. I would like every hotel in
> every city to be trained. When the Super Bowl comes to
> town, everybody trains the cab drivers, and they train the
> hotels, and they train the workers at the airport, and they
> train all of these people, but just because it's the Super
> Bowl—this happens in every city across the United States
> when a large event comes to town. It doesn't have to be
> the Super Bowl or just a sporting event. It could be a large

business convention. It could be anything, and the cities need to be trained. So, yes, I've seen progress and I'm looking very forward to what's to come in the future.

Importantly, this respondent noted that hotels were used to sell sex when large groups of men were expected to be in town for a variety of different reasons. Consequently, limiting hotel training to large sporting events is not sufficient to prevent or identify sex trafficking situations. St. Louis has a large convention center downtown, and Collinsville, IL, just fifteen minutes from downtown St. Louis, also has a large convention center. Both of these centers draw hundreds of thousands of people each year for various business and entertainment endeavors. Further, the St. Louis airport also draws millions of visitors each year. Multiple prosecuted cases and cases described by survivors and social service providers have involved the hotels near the St. Louis airport. Consequently, training hotel staff in these key areas can work to provide identification and possibly prevention of a sex trafficking situation. The director of The Exchange Initiative also pointed out:

> .... we were first in conference and meeting management and our company took a corporate stand against sex trafficking, because we work in hotels across the United States and globally. We realized that when large events would come to town that would be a red light for traffickers to bring in girls. And we had the ability that when we went into the hotel we could have a conversation with the hotel, bring awareness to the fact that sex trafficking does happen, show them that their hotels can be featured on websites like Back Page.com. And we decided that this was going to be our corporate social responsibility and we were going to do this in every hotel that we visited and utilized ... we could go on these internet sites like Back Page.com and recognize the hotel rooms, because we had been in so many of the meeting planning companies, we could recognize the throws, we could recognize the bedding, we could recognize the things outside.

The sex-for-sale advertisements commonly posted online, of which at least a portion of the ads involve sex trafficking victims, are often taken in hotels. This is corroborated by multiple prosecuted cases of sex-trafficking related charges nationwide, as well as accounts of survivors and the reports of social service providers who directly work with survivors in the St. Louis area (see Nichols & Heil, 2014; Heil & Nichols, 2014). In fact, as depicted in the example above, hotel workers are able to identify which hotels the pictures in the ads were taken in based on the décor depicted in the photos (Nichols & Heil, 2014). Such trainings work to raise awareness of hotel staff. For example, in-call sex trafficking may involve multiple people coming and going to the same room, and staying one at a time for short periods (an hour or less) of time. Out-call sex trafficking may involve a returning hotel customer (the sex-trafficked individual) who checks in for short periods of time on different dates with different guests each time (Nichols, 2015; End Slavery Cincinnati, 2014). When hotel staff are trained in these and other potential warning signs, it increases the likelihood of identification.

In addition, on-the-ground workers, such as postal workers, plumbers, electric, phone, and cable company workers, as well as Fire Marshal and Code Compliance officers were identified as those who worked on-the-ground, in largely door to door occupations, who may see suspicious activity. The Rescue and Restore coalition worked to train such individuals to identify labor and sex trafficking. For example, the director of Rescue and Restore St. Louis stated:

> But we are also branching out into talking to individuals who are in a capacity of going inside people's homes, or like the Post Office was a brand new one that we hadn't talked about before, but these are people who are in the community on a very regular basis and if given the proper training would know what they were looking at if they saw it, because they've probably come across it, and thought, 'Oh, something weird is going on there.' And they don't have the name for it and don't know what to do about it. So, we're branching out into that. And these are going to be people, again, who have no background in any kind of

social service work, or in human trafficking knowledge. And so, a part of it is getting them that basic knowledge, and then, the indicators and then what to do about it.

The Rescue and Restore St. Louis coalition used the Polaris project training materials for training fire marshals and code compliance officers, but also extended this training to plumbers, Ameren UE (electricity services) employees, and Charter (cable company) employees, as well as postal workers. The training ended with a "what to do" approach under suspicious circumstances, including reporting a tip to the NHTRC hotline, contacting law enforcement, and importantly, "documenting and photographing all observations and activities," as this could potentially be used as important evidence (Rescue and Restore, 2014).

Remaining Gaps in Training

While training was described as a major strength in the St. Louis area, with lots of activity occurring by multiple groups, respondents also noted that the training was incomplete. This indicates that it is important for training to be ongoing. For example, one social service provider noted, "There's just a huge thing with front line staff not having training." The executive director of The Covering House noted that more frontline workers needed training as well: "Probably what's lacking—more services, certainly I think training for police officers and other healthcare professionals and other first responders." While many trainings were conducted, many more trainings were still needed. Importantly, a few individuals were largely conducting all of the trainings in the greater St. Louis area. Social service providers also noted that training was incomplete across the region, and there were some gaps in training among front-line workers likely to come into contact with sex trafficking victims. As described in Chapter Four, training of law enforcement was inconsistent across jurisdictions. Officers' access to training, and perceptions of sex trafficking, varied widely across the bi-state region. Similarly, training across the various service sectors was also incomplete. For example, one social service provider stated:

> Social services are a long way from having their training, enough training for everybody inside of the state system in Missouri.

Other social service providers indicated key areas that were still in need of training, such as those who worked answering crisis line calls, and child protective services:

> With social services, so everywhere that there's awareness of the problem, of course we need to train. I also think that extends to crisis lines. So, our crisis lines we have really great crisis lines in town, but training and awareness of human trafficking especially sex trafficking in our area, is not, it's just not really there.

Another social service provider working with foster kids maintained:

> A thousand percent I think that we need specific trafficking services. And I'm seeing that firsthand working for a branch of children's division. We're incredibly limited, as far as that goes. We don't get training in trafficking. We don't have any therapists that specialize in trafficking. We don't have any kind of manuals that describe "these are the behaviors to see in trafficking victims."

Consequently, ongoing training and continued funding of education, awareness, and training campaigns may be important in continuing anti-trafficking efforts.

Another key point is that in the St. Louis area, turnover in the St. Louis Police department, and also social workers in the broader community, particularly in child protective services, is very high. As a result, trainings within the same organizations may be needed multiple times, or included as part of the initial hiring process, to address the high turnover. In addition to community awareness and training of those who may come into contact with survivors, direct outreach was also identified as a strategy to increase identification of human trafficking survivors.

Direct Outreach

The Rescue and Restore Coalitions of St. Louis and Southwestern Illinois have multiple ongoing subcommittees, projects, and trainings that work to increase identification of victims through direct outreach. This includes providing information about resources and advertising the national hotline on billboards, local newspapers, and disseminating flyers in neighborhoods, among others. The aim is to provide information in areas where survivors may come into contact with this posted information. One example of an outreach project involved disseminating the National Human Trafficking Hotline to both labor trafficking and sex trafficking victims, placing products in places victims are more likely to come into contact with them. For example, the Coalitions recently developed a plan to place sanitary napkins in hotels and in truck stop restrooms. These places have been identified in the existing research literature, and among prosecuted cases, as hot spots for sex trafficking to occur (Kotrla, 2010; Nichols & Heil, 2014). The sanitary napkins do not have the hotline in a place visible on the outside of the packaging, as this could present a danger to the victim if the trafficker saw it. Rather, the hotline number, along with other brief information about trafficking, is placed "fortune-cookie-style" inserted within the applicator of each individually wrapped tampon, and the information can be flushed down the toilet safely. The information is printed in both English and Spanish, and aims at targeting females who may be engaged in sex trafficking or labor trafficking. This particular project would not aid in the identification of males; however, additional dissemination in the form of toothbrushes, bars of soap, and chapstick were also presented as possibilities in order to assist male victims of sex or labor trafficking. With toothbrushes and chapstick, the idea was that the items were small and ordinary, and not likely to be closely scrutinized by a trafficker. The items were also not disposable and the survivors would have continued access to the information if she or he decided to seek assistance.

As in community education and training, some gaps were identified in direct outreach as well. These gaps largely included outreach involving the immigrant population, as well as outreach to potential victims of labor trafficking (described in Chapter Two). For example, the director of Rescue and Restore St. Louis described how the gap in outreach to immigrants was identified, and the response of the coalition to work to address it:

> So the Immigrant Service Provider Group [subcommittee of Rescue and Restore] kind of started because this coalition was getting so big that certain needs of the immigrant population they felt weren't being met well enough by everybody, and that's understandable when you get 20 to 25 people at a table with different backgrounds. So the Immigrant Service Provider Group meets to address issues specific to the immigrant community. What they do is they target a particular community. So rather than trying to reach all ethnic groups at one time, we pick a group that hasn't had any outreach maybe or a group that we think we have enough contacts in to sort of actually make a difference. We use that to bring awareness to that community. We've put a little editorial in an ethnic newsletter for the Philippines, they have their own little, not a welcome group, but they have their own network that provides a newsletter to the Filipino community here in the United States, in St. Louis. And we approached the editors of that particular letter and they said you can write something. So, we wrote a little short piece about human trafficking and what it might look like in their community, and what they could do about it, and put that in. So we reach out into different ways that we think that particular ethnic community is going to listen. And then we've done things like gone to certain festivals. So, we went to the Asian Heritage Festival and set up a table and had different resources for people to take. We've gone to the first Kerala Festival from an Indian Community. So we pay attention to those kinds of things that are very general.

The director also indicated a plan-in-progress to conduct outreach and facilitate identification through service providers most likely to encounter labor or sex trafficking victims:

> ... we also talk about training service providers of one kind or another who serve immigrant populations. So, going to places like Casa De Salud and training the health-care workers there. Training interpreters, so since many of these immigrants need interpreters for any of the services that they request, they often have to have an interpreter. So, we have a new initiative through the International Institute where there is a training specific for interpreters in how to recognize when someone they're helping interpret for is showing signs of human trafficking. And then, protocols what to do about that ... so if there's some questions that are going back and forth and the immigrant says something like, 'I'm not being paid, or I'm not being paid what was said, or what they told me.' So that's an indicator for the interpreter. The reason we want to make interpreters aware is because maybe that professional doesn't know. So if the professional doesn't pick up on those same indicators, then the interpreter can pick that up and leave a tip in the appropriate place. So, or ... if they say something like, if it's a sex trafficking victim and they say something like, 'Well, I have to make money for my boyfriend.' 'He needs me to help him pay the bills.' That kind of a thing. So, those are some indicators. If they talk about the last time they had a meal was two days ago, or 24 hours, or something like that, these are red flags that we would hope the professional knows about, but they might not. So we also want to train the interpreter to recognize that, and then ... so we have these kind of checks and balances and more than one avenue for victims to be rescued.

Accordingly, outreach to and identification of immigrant populations and labor trafficking victims was viewed as an area in need of improvement, and a plan was in place to address it. At the time of this writing, a sub-committee, the Immigrant Service Provider group, was formed to work to address this gap.

In addition to outreach to and identification of labor trafficking victims, social services were also found to be limited for labor trafficking victims. According to the respondents in this study, two organizations in the St. Louis bi-state area were largely credited with offering services to labor trafficking survivors. The International Institute "manages and supports the Eastern Missouri and Southern Illinois Rescue and Restore Consortium. The Consortium is comprised of 4 coalitions that conduct outreach and education with the ultimate goal of identifying victims. In addition, social workers are able to provide comprehensive case management for foreign born victims and referral services for all victims" (IISTL, 2013). Legal service of Eastern Missouri (LSEM) provides civil legal services for low income individuals, including services related to immigration and/or trafficking. LSEM represents both U.S. citizens and qualified non-citizens, and close relatives of U.S. citizens. Outside of these organization, which provided legal and social services, and the community awareness, outreach, and training efforts of the Rescue and Restore coalitions, described above and in Chapter Two, social services were primarily focused upon sex trafficking survivors. Consequently, Chapter Six exclusively describes social service provision for sex trafficking survivors.

In sum, efforts toward identification through community awareness, training, and direct outreach were generally described as successful. Respondents noted ongoing and expanded training and community awareness were necessary to maintain the momentum of the anti-trafficking movement, and to increase identification. Respondents also worked to identify gaps in these areas as well, and created plans to address such gaps. The Rescue and Restore Coalition worked to solicit responses from the community related to perceived gaps. Subcommittees were developed on order to cultivate further plans for identification and outreach. In particular, labor trafficking and immigrant outreach were delineated as important areas in need of further attention, with subcommittees actively focused on improving these areas at the time of the writing of this manuscript. In addition to education, training, and outreach, community based responses also include collaboration between various anti-trafficking organizations.

Collaboration

The TVPA emphasized collaboration between law enforcement and social service providers, with the goal of streamlined services for survivors. Collaboration was described as both a benefit and a challenge in the St. Louis area. The primary challenge to collaboration was that connections were disjointed. There were multiple forms of informal and formal connections, but there didn't appear to be a broader connection between various community partners. This lack of organized collaboration led to the research findings that some individuals found collaboration in St. Louis to be highly successful, but others found it to be problematic. Consequently, collaboration with community partners was also described as an area of progress in St. Louis, but as an area in need of improvement as well. Benefits of collaboration included informal connections and relationships that worked on behalf of survivors, as well as better understandings of one another's programs, goals, and needs. Challenges to collaboration included lack of formal channels and being unsure of who to call for what particular need.

Informal Connections

A majority of respondents indicated that informal connections were important in providing services for trafficking victims. The director of The Magdalene House, a program for adult women, indicated that the program's waiting list was lengthy, and she needed to draw from community connections in order to provide some level of assistance for such individuals:

> I have a much better handle on who I can call when I get a phone call. We get them every day. We have a waiting list of women who want to come into the program ... so, working with the other service providers is invaluable right now, but again, I feel like it's, you hear someone's

story over the phone or you go and meet them, or you hear their stories, okay I'm going to call this person, I'm going to call that person, because you figure out what the needs might be of that particular individual ...

Another respondent working in the Juvenile Division of the Family Courts in St. Louis noted the importance of informal connections, specifically, knowing who to call to get placements for kids:

Well, for example, we have agencies that are state approved to keep kids, and I know quite a few of them, they are willing if we call and say, 'Hey we have a kid who has had these experiences, can you keep this kid temporarily until we can find out more about what's going on,' I mean 99% of the time they're like, 'Oh, fine.' If we call another one that is more secure, we say that this kid is a runner ... 'Oh, we'll work with that.' Or sometimes we may have to place a kid away from St. Louis because it's for safety concerns, and they are willing to work with us.

These two examples are representative of typical responses of the research participants—there were informal relationships that they drew from in order to network and access resources for sex trafficking survivors.

Another social service provider who worked with youth services indicated that collaboration was not only desirable, but necessary in order to best provide for survivors:

I mean the main benefit is that like none of us can do this on our own, you know, and no matter how magnificent your agency is, we do have a limited number of beds, we do have a limited number of staff, and so to make sure that we're really reaching as many kids as possible, I think that it is imperative that we collaborate. I think the challenges mostly are finding ways to really effectively communicate, and then, funding resources, because you know, I may have a kid from St. Louis City and the only opening is at an agency who can only take St. Louis

County kids. And so, running into those kinds of barriers just because of a zip code is really a huge, huge challenge.

The same individual also noted the importance of various professional community groups and the St. Louis Rescue and Restore coalition in this collaboration:

And then, there are different understandings and perceptions and levels of awareness and training that have been done across agencies on these topics of commercial sexual exploitation, and so, I think making sure that we are kind of a unified front in this movement versus kind of all siloed into our experiences and our perceptions. So the more we can streamline how we view and how we approach these kids, because consistency is so huge for them, and it's a huge piece of doing trauma-informed care ... I think iron sharpens iron and I would like to think that that is what a lot of these agencies in the region are doing is really spurring each other on and realizing that we don't ... no one agency has the answer, like we all need each other and thankfully there are a lot of collaborative groups whether it's a shelter workgroup meeting, or a Rescue Restore Coalition, there are a lot of places that we can go and share information and build relationships with each other.

While recognizing the importance of these informal relationships, as well as available avenues conducive to collaboration, some respondents indicated that more formalized connections would be an improvement.

Formal Connections

The development of formal connections was described as an area in-progress in the anti-trafficking community. The director of The Exchange Initiative illustrated:

They [informal relationships] are very important. I would like to see them be more formalized, and we're all sort of working on that right now, about how we work together … and what our intention is in terms of being a coalition, why are we doing what we're doing other than to network. Are we doing this so that we can be a united voice when it comes to talking to the police department when it comes to going to Jefferson City is that our goal? I don't think we're there yet.

Many respondents noted that collaboration was important, as different agencies in the St. Louis area specialized in different areas. Yet, some social service providers reported not knowing the appropriate contacts, or how or when to reach them:

I think the collaboration, I think, is the big thing, collaboration, long-term, looking at it holistically. What are all of the pieces? So I think we can't offer all of those things [various types of services], obviously, different organizations can offer all of those things. So, how do we use the resources that are available? I don't necessarily have to be an expert in everything. I need to know where the resources are, so I think that's kind of missing. Is that I know that there are a lot of resources in St. Louis, but how do you find those resources and utilize them the best way?

Another respondent indicated the same sentiment:

I think we're getting there. There is intent for collaboration I just don't think we've figured out how to do it completely yet, if that's fair? I think the collaboration piece, like I said I think people want that to happen, I just don't think it has happened yet, maybe because we're in such a big city it's hard to know what resources are available. It's hard to know who is doing what and who's doing what well … Sometimes it feel like there is kind of reinventing the wheel because we don't know what somebody else is doing, or we're getting asked to do things that are not necessarily in our specific demographic. And we know that there are people doing it, it's just hard to know where those pieces fall together.

She illustrated that the St. Louis area is rather large, and there are a large number of organizations providing a myriad of social services. Attaining the knowledge of each of these, and to draw formal and informal connections in St. Louis, and the bi-state area, was a bit daunting for some. Collaboration between anti-trafficking groups was indicated as a developing area, with some "inside the loop" and others "outside the loop."

In order to address the issue of formalized connections, some organizations were working through formal channels to develop a service provider handbook. This handbook has lists of community organizations, what services they offer, and contact information. The Human Trafficking Manual for Social Service Providers also contains a review of legal processes, including flowcharts, for both labor and sex trafficking. This was an effort to develop more formalized connections, and to disseminate this information across social service agencies in the area. In addition, a group called the Exchange Initiative worked to connect the anti-trafficking community through formal channels as well. The director illustrated:

> There are many benefits to working with coalitions. In the St. Louis area, we have the most non-profits in the United States, right here … but everybody is fighting trafficking and everybody does something different. And so, where I can provide information and network groups together, they may not have networked before, so the prosecutor's office may not have known to go to the YWCA to provide services for someone, or a school who is in desperate need of educating their at-risk youth, or really their youth period, may not know that they can go to Rescue and Restore and get a program, or as we work together with Congress to provide stronger legislation to fight trafficking, we can network survivors and have new projects that we can all work together to build a strong force against them.

Other organizations were working on developing their own formal connections. For example, the director of The Covering House, which provides services to sex-trafficked or sexually exploited girls, stated:

> About six months ago when we were getting ready moving forward opening the house, and we were doing some different things, I said Lindsey let's set up meetings with family courts, case managers, law enforcement, health providers, and say this is what we're doing, what do you need? What can we do to help you? Where is the biggest gap? Because if we can help with that, we want to fill that.

Similarly, the Juvenile Division of the Family Courts in St. Louis City was active in developing formal connections:

> Well, I know ... you can't do this job alone. And in realizing that we convened several meetings on our end, not that we have the answers, but we know the different organizations and community partners are addressing the same thing ... so we attempted to bring folks together and say, 'Okay, what are you doing and how can we help you?' And share how they can help us. So, we've reached out to hospitals and doctors seeing these girls come in for injuries or STD's or pregnancies. We've reached out to all of our partner agencies that are associated with Children's Division. We've reached out to some of the health providers and some of the residential facilities that are having to house some of these girls. We're also a part of a few initiatives, that's another way that we can partner, and it's been great ... we work with Rescue and Restore Coalition, both 'Jim' and I are a part of the U.S. Attorney's Office Trafficking Task Force, so I think that has been really good because before we were involved in all of these things, we had no idea where to start or what to do, or how big this was, but when you talk to all of these people that are dealing with it, it's been good to know that there are folks that are working on this as well.

An additional benefit to working collaboratively with organizations whose goals appeared to be different from one another was that such organizations could recognize a shared goal. For example, the goal of law enforcement is to "get the bad guy" whereas the goal for social service providers is to assist survivors. Recognizing the role of each in an ultimate goal of addressing sex trafficking was imperative to cooperation and collaboration. The director of Rescue and Restore St. Louis stated:

> So what happens is they get the idea that they're [law enforcement and social services] actually working against each other. And so, when they come to this table there's an opportunity for each to begin to understanding the other. And then, realize that we're not working against each other, we're actually on the same side, we're just coming from a different angle, and that becomes important in all that we do. And the other benefit is similar to that it's just that you have to have a multitude of voices or your answers to the problem are lopsided and can cause some consequences that you didn't anticipate. So, those latent consequences can be really devastating if you don't have the victim's voice. If you don't have the shelter voices, if you don't have a corporate voice. All of these people come with how is something going to service what I do, or how is something going to negate what I do, and then, that helps us build a better ... that's kind of the beauty of working with so many different people is that we learn from each other and we kind of make other connections click that hadn't happened before.

The development of informal and formal connections helped to increase understandings of each groups' work, recognition of a shared goal, knowledge of available community resources and organizations, and ultimately, collaboration.

The research findings additionally suggest collaboration between anti-trafficking stakeholders and other organizations in the community. For example, some respondents indicated that the justice system worked collaboratively with schools. Working with a truancy list provided by schools, as well as working with a list of chronic runaways may also be helpful to law enforcement to address prevention of sex trafficking, as runaway and truant youth are at an increased risk (see Chapter Three). Respondents working

in the Juvenile Division of the Family Courts in St. Louis City indicated that they "might have 60 to 70 names on the list" at any
given time, and these cases often involved sex trafficking.

> So, going back to the list … if a child runs away so many
> times we would have it on the list. So sometimes we
> would have a kid on the list and if the kid was 16 and then
> three years later we might hear on the news, oh, this
> young lady from … was caught in another state and she
> runaway … and she ran to the police and she was being
> kept against her will, and I look at the list and I say, 'Dr.
> Lampley, did you know that she was on the list?' And I
> said, 'Yeah, that's her name, she was on the list, but she's
> 19 now.' But she said she was kept against her will in an-
> other state and she had a child or something like that, but
> she was on the list …

This example indicates that in addition to a truancy list, a list of
chronic runaways was also pointed out as a fruitful avenue for
identifying at-risk youth for sex trafficking. Accordingly, collaboration between schools, parents, the juvenile division, and social
service providers would create a streamlined flow of identification
through service provision.

Chapter Summary

In sum, various organizations in the St. Louis bi-state area
worked to increase awareness of labor and sex trafficking. Community awareness, training of professionals, and direct outreach
efforts aimed to increase identification and gain public and political support for trafficked people. These areas were consistently described by research participants as "what's working" in the St.
Louis area anti-trafficking movement. At the same time, respondents described outreach among immigrant populations as in need
of further work. In addition, the emphasis on labor trafficking was
generally limited throughout. Moreover, formal channels of collaboration were also described as in need of further development.

Further, collaboration with anti-trafficking stakeholders and other community organizations, such as schools, offered an important implication for prevention and identification.

Chapter 6

Social Service Provision for
Sex Trafficking Survivors

In the previous chapter, we discussed the roles of social service providers as they provide education and training to the community, as well as the collaborative efforts between law enforcement, social service providers, and the community. However, through our research, we found the experiences of identified sex trafficking survivors to be unique. Because of the trauma, guilt, and self-blame of many of the survivors, it is crucial that survivors receive various avenues of support as they struggle through the healing process after being identified as a victim of sex trafficking. In spite of lack of funding, social service providers in St. Louis and the bi-state area have found the means to house, clothe, educate, and provide trauma care to survivors from the moment of identification to what can only be called social and psychological independence. This support for survivors is crucial, for without it, many survivors will return to their trafficker or suffer from long-term trauma effects. Consequently, it is important to examine the work of social service providers and the vital role these various groups play in the lives of sex trafficking survivors.

Chapter Six examines the work of social service organizations that directly assist survivors of trafficking. Expansion of available services was described as a successful avenue of progress. Yet, gaps were identified within these areas that needed to be addressed. For example, progress was made in the development of transitional housing and shelter for sex-trafficked adults and minor girls, but shelter space was still not nearly enough to meet the demand from these groups, and available shelter explicitly for sex-trafficked boys and LGBTQ youth was found to be absent. Moreover, services that were trauma-informed, survivor-informed, and designed specifically for sex trafficking survivors were delineated as extremely important to the recovery of survivors, but were limited in relationship to the need for such services. The social service provision responses that were found to be successful, those that offer promising directions for social work practice, and responses or services that presented challenges or were lacking are examined in detail in the following sections.

The Need for Sex-Trafficking-Specific Services

Training in identification, as well as efforts toward outreach, is very different from the expertise needed to work specifically with sex trafficking survivors. In fact, respondents consistently stated that targeted services for sex trafficking survivors provided by experts specially trained in working with them was necessary. The respondents in this study made it clear that it is important to offer sex trafficking-specific services because of survivors' distinct experiences and outcomes. Currently, such services are limited across the nation; there are relatively few programs for minors and adult women nationwide. There are only three programs in the entire Midwest that provide for girls between the ages of thirteen and seventeen, and only one in the entire state of Missouri which is limited to eight beds.

When a sex trafficking survivor is identified, the options are to attempt to get into one of these programs or to use local resources. Both of these options present challenges. First, to get into one of the few programs exclusively for sex trafficking survivors is difficult, because there are few of them, space is limited, and the waiting lists are long. Simply put, the demand for such services far exceeds the availability. Second, using alternative services in the area, such as juvenile detention, rehabilitation, mental hospitals, domestic violence shelters, or foster care is problematic for multiple reasons. Sex trafficking survivors experience unique trauma that requires services and expertise that specifically considers this trauma and uses it as a centerpiece of therapeutic techniques. Further, survivors may not recognize their victimization, or even label themselves as a "victim" or "survivor" until years after their abuse when they are able to understand and come to terms with what happened to them. Expertise of service providers in sex trafficking, recognizing the multiple forms trafficking takes, and the varied needs of each individual survivor based upon these forms and even the different techniques of pimps is important in working with sex trafficking survivors. In addition, girls who do not get appropriate treatment may recruit other girls for their pimp. Consequently, it is not appropriate for trafficking survivors to be placed in juvenile detention, group homes, or other facilities where other higher-risk girls would be in jeopardy of recruitment into prostitution. Moreover, in such settings, service provision by those specifically educated in practices related to sex trafficking is less likely to be present. Girls may also be further revictimized by being treated as delinquent or mentally ill in detention or rehabilitation centers. In sum, service provision by those with expertise in working with sex trafficking survivors is imperative because of their unique trauma, disconnect from victimization, risk of revictimization and running from services, and risk to others in non-sex-trafficking-specific settings. The following subsections highlight each of these.

Unique Trauma

Sex-trafficking-related trauma is distinct, in that the trauma is repeated multiple times, often several times a day, over an extended period of time. In many cases, the trauma is facilitated by someone who the victim loves, and believes returns that love. The seemingly dichotomous relationship between love and repeated trauma are conflated in the experiences of sex trafficking survivors, making it a somewhat unique form of trauma. When asked if specialized services were important in working with clients, one social service provider described how trauma was unique in the case of sex trafficking survivors:

> Trafficking victims endure a lot of physical and psychological abuse on a repeated basis, and that's kind of where

the complex trauma comes from. So they're not just abused one time, and they're not abused by just anybody. They're abused multiple times over and over again, by someone who is supposed to be their caregiver.

Multiple social service providers, who worked with survivors, and survivors themselves, delineated similar statements. The executive director of The Covering House, who worked with girls under 18, described how trauma experienced by sex trafficking survivors was distinct in terms of repeated trauma and trauma enacted by a loved one. She depicted the way sex-trafficking-related trauma was different from other forms of trauma using the examples of domestic violence and sexual abuse to comparatively illustrate:

> Domestic violence, while it may play out [similar to sex trafficking] in terms of physical abuse and some control, the differences are the girls that have gone through this have dealt with very complex trauma, when you are asked to service on minimum 20 men a day, the trauma that they've endured not just at the hands of their pimp, but the Johns is in some cases mind boggling. There's one case for sure I don't even know how she physically survived it. And so the trauma looks the same in some aspects, it's different in others, and a big portion of it too is trust and building trust, because when you've been in this situation for a long time and the person that you put your trust in, being the pimp, thinking he's going to take care of you, he's going to love you, he's my boyfriend, whatever, my daddy, however they identify with him, then he sells you, rents you out and that sort of thing, and if you don't, then, walk the line all of the physical and emotional and especially the psychological abuse that occurs from him, from the other girls that are in that situation that are a part of that culture, as well as the men who are purchasing—just shatters the trust for these girls. Where a girl who has been sexually abused by a family member, still tragic, still needs help, they may not have their trust shattered for every person that they come in contact with, and

certainly not every man that they've come in contact with, but for these girls they have been abused 20 times a day from 20 different men. Even their outlook and view on men is going to be so skewed towards fear of them that it sets them apart from people who have been abused in domestic violence.

This example demarcates the importance of the role of both pimps and clients in sex trafficking related trauma, not just in the repeated commercial sexual exchanges, but also noting the relationship between this trauma and trust. The exploitation, abuse, and violence are not perpetrated by only one person, as in a specific domestic violence or sexual assault situation. In sex trafficking, such dynamics involve multiple people over periods of time. Sex trafficking survivors may have difficulty building trust with any man, as the men in their lives largely included clients and pimps who exploited or abused them. Consequently, sex-trafficking-specific services are needed to address the dynamics inherent to sex trafficking related trauma, particularly in terms of building trust and addressing repeated trauma.

A survivor also noted how important it was to understand such trauma, and why sex-trafficking-specific services were necessary to address not only trust, but issues such as PTSD and Stockholm Syndrome (e.g., trauma bonds) as well:

Right now what they do.... unfortunately women leaving the streets they get put in a domestic violence shelter ... that's not appropriate. They're not in a domestic violence situation, [or] maybe there might be domestic violence involved—they may have developed a relationship with their pimp, but it's not the same. It's not the holistic services. When we're dealing with trauma bonding, or I guess we used to call it Stockholm Syndrome, and Post Traumatic Stress, I mean the heightened Post Traumatic Stress, we know that rape is part of the daily work hazards. It's not just sex, I mean, men pay to rape women. The violence and the physical abuse by strangers, and you know the "fight or flight," or just depending on their own individual survivor skills day after day after day ... we [survivors] need more intensified services.

Importantly, she noted the dynamics of love for the pimp/trafficker in the language of Stockholm Syndrome, and PTSD from prostitution, which was viewed as multiple daily rapes in the eyes of this survivor, as well as being in a constant state of survival mode. Many of these things are related to the "fight or flight" characteristics typical of trauma survivors. Fight or flight refers to the biological processes of "survival mode" that become hard-wired in a trauma survivor's brain, where the individual literally flees a situation or may become combative or aggressive when triggered. Ostensibly, holistic, sex-trafficking-specific services are necessary in order to address these unique forms of trauma, and the long-term effects of "fight or flight," PTSD, and trauma-bonds with the trafficker.

Some respondents indicated further understandings of trauma and sex trafficking were needed in various social service agencies. One social service provider provided a typical response:

> I think a lot of our agencies are really working on cultural competency and that is really great, but what we are really missing is understanding of, not just like what trauma is but how do we go about implementing trauma informed care, and trauma informed consequences ... because when these youth get into our care, like I said, they are not the perfect victims ... they can be very challenging to work with. And no matter how many degrees you have or how clinical you are, sometimes we don't know the best way to work with them in ways that don't further harm them, re-traumatize them and actually help them grow and build new skills. So, I think more conversation around that needs to occur, because trafficking and trauma are like one and the same, basically. I don't think there's any way you can get out of a trafficking situation and not have some kind of trauma.

Importantly, this example illustrates that survivors do not always fit the image of the perfect victim, and advocating for their goals and needs can be challenging. Trauma-informed therapy can be vital in addressing the fight or flight responses that some sex trafficking survivors may exhibit, and which provide challenges to helping them. Recovery is not usually simply a matter of "rescue" from sex trafficking situations. When asked what was needed in social services in St. Louis, a social service provider indicated a need for trauma-informed practice, and related this to why some girls run from services:

> I think the unresolved trauma [is missing from practice]. Agencies are doing a lot of good, but are not as trauma informed as they need to be. And so a youth gets triggered, a youth feels unsafe, something happens and they don't feel welcome, they feel unsure of a lot of different things there. And I think they would go back to maybe what they know, or they just go into fight or flight response. And they need to get out, and even though it's a safe wonderful space maybe that they're in, it doesn't feel like it in that moment, or they want freedom.

Ostensibly, trauma-informed sex-trafficking-specific services may be a promising avenue for practice in working with survivors. Understanding the multifaceted nature of sex trafficking and the related trauma is imperative to understand in order to best provide services. Further, trauma-informed therapy may prevent survivors from running away from services that are not sex-trafficking-specific by addressing "fight or flight" responses to triggering events, as well as trauma-bonds with the trafficker (e.g., pimp).

Ineffectiveness of Non-Sex-Trafficking-Specific Services

When asked about best practices, many respondents indicated that they couldn't say for sure what worked, but they could say what didn't work—non-sex-trafficking-specific services. This message was stated consistently across interviews from individuals across multiple areas, such as foster care, the juvenile division, child protective services, youth services, and direct services to trafficked or exploited individuals. Because few options were available

for sex-trafficked youth, typical responses included use of local resources, which varied across the Illinois/Missouri bi-state area,
such as foster care placements, juvenile detention, or residential
care in mental hospitals or rehabilitation centers. These settings
were found to be problematic for a number of reasons.

First, a respondent from the Juvenile Division of the Family
Courts in St. Louis indicated that one of the things that didn't
work was simply placing a trafficked youth in foster care:

> I think a lot of facilities ... the people cannot address
> those issues because a lot of places don't know how to ad-
> dress those issues. There's not a traditional methodology
> with it [working with trafficking survivors]. So you have
> some facilities that are focusing on that, because if you
> place a kid who has been sex trafficked with a regular fos-
> ter care kid, they're completely out of place. So, you have
> to have special [services].

When a youth is placed in foster care, they may or may not access
additional services. Further, the services that are accessed may not be
sex-trafficking specific or trauma-informed. As a result, sex-trafficked
youth placed in foster care may not be getting the help they need. In
fact, chronic runaways were associated with sex trafficking survivors
placed in foster care. Consequently, placement in foster care was described as problematic in addressing sex trafficking victimization.

Multiple respondents indicated that services specifically for sex
trafficking survivors were a better option as opposed to being
housed in a foster placement, juvenile detention, rehabilitation,
mental hospitals, or domestic violence services. One social service
provider elaborated on why sex-trafficking-specific services were
better than non-sex-trafficking-specific services:

> I think, you know, services are really recently starting to
> fill in those gaps, as far as trafficking-specific services; be-
> cause while we treat the symptoms, we're not treating the
> actual cause. So we would treat she's a runner, she's a self-
> harmer, she's ... so we treat those, but we wouldn't treat
> the actual trafficking ...

Importantly, this respondent noted that the trafficking often went unaddressed in responses to sex trafficking victimization. Further, the director of the Juvenile Division also indicated that sex-trafficking-specific services were preferred in order to prevent kids from running from services:

> I mean, foster care will place ... we can place the child, but the issue is not being addressed. I mean you might have ... they might be in therapy but we've seen that with kids who have gone into foster care and just gotten therapy, general therapy, and they still locked them ... and they still run. And they go back to that same lifestyle ... not all of the time but many times they do. So I think it needs to be very targeted and specific.

Notably, non-sex-trafficking-specific services were identified as ineffective in treating the root source of the problem, frequently leading to runaway status and re-trafficking, potentially due to trauma bonds with the trafficker or the "flight" response typical of trauma survivors. One social service provider who had prior experience working in residential facilities, and who currently worked as director of operations at The Covering House, was in a position to contrast non-specialized and specialized services. She maintained:

> Being in residential [facilities], the hard part is when you're dealing with minors, is that a lot of times you have a group of kids that are all thrown together and they're all focused on different things. So you have ... you might have a therapist or staff or whoever is working with them and you have all of these different niches that they have to try to do. Where having a specific group, our whole focus is on one thing. So we have an overarching program that also allows us to be very individualistic with our programming. So we can take this overarching thing of here's we're doing safety, we're working on trauma, we're reconnecting them. And, we have these three overarching things that their programming can be very individualized and

their context of that. And having that understanding of all of the girls ... like for example, we're talking to a lot of girls right now that are in other residential and then they're not bad, but they [survivors] automatically feel like an outsider because the other girls don't understand what they've been through; because they're all there for different reasons. You might talk to a different girl that has a completely different thing than our girls and they might say the same thing, because they're walking through a completely different issue, or circumstance, than what the clients we're working with are. So it just allows them ... we're very big on group counseling ... and it allows them to all kind of walk in with a certain level of trust already built without having to feel judged. They automatically have an acceptance to a degree just because they've walked through something similar.

Significantly, when services are not sex-trafficking-specific, survivors may be placed in facilities with individuals who are accessing services for different reasons. This could include anger management issues, perpetrating violent crimes, substance abuse, or other things that may or may not apply to a sex-trafficked person. In a non-trafficking-specific setting, trafficked people are getting help for problems they may not have, and are not getting help for the problems that they do have. A typical response to address trafficked girls who repeatedly run away and return to their trafficker is to apply lock-down care. Yet the other girls in such facilities may be in for a myriad of other issues unrelated to trafficking. Further, addressing the reasons for running away are not sufficiently addressed in non-sex-trafficking-specific settings.

Why Do Girls Run from Services?

Importantly, because of not getting the care that they needed, girls often ran away from social services to go back to "what they know." Accordingly, girls who were "rescued" often engaged in a revolving door taking them right back to the streets. While some survivors interviewed for this book were confined, locked in a room, kept under surveillance, or otherwise prevented from leaving forced prostitution, this occurred in a minority of cases. Others did not define themselves as victims, and wanted to return to their trafficker or to street life. This was particularly the case with minors who had been manipulated by a pimp-as-boyfriend. In fact, once girls had been "rescued" they often returned to the streets. When asked, "So do you see a lot of girls running from services?" One respondent working with juveniles in the family courts in St. Louis City enthusiastically stated, "Yes! Yes! Yes!" When further prompted with, "Why do you think they leave?" he responded:

> The lure, the drive. I don't want to say a false sense of freedom, which it probably is, because they're making money, and how should I say, it's a false sense of security, we have somebody say, 'Get your hair done, get your manicure,' 'You dress nice.' You're making money, but you're not getting the money! So I think it's the lure that you are on your own and you can get drugs and alcohol. I think all of that is all tied into using them and the drugs and things like that. So it's hard to get young ladies to stop ...

In this case, the respondent noted that girls initially liked the attention and the material items from pimps, and being able to participate in a partying lifestyle, and often returned to the streets to maintain independence. He noted that they were not getting the care they needed to prevent chronic runaway status.

Another social service provider in mental health stated that kids needed to feel independent, and that they needed to have choices, or they would run:

> Kids, you can't make them do what you want them to do, if they want to run they are going to run. On the streets they felt independent, and able to pick and choose who they went with, what they didn't want was to be locked into a residential ward where they couldn't leave and they were controlled.

This example illustrates that lock-down facilities can be viewed as revictimizing by taking away survivors' control and freedom, which may be retraumatizing. Similarly, another respondent working with child services described working with a fourteen-year-old trafficking survivor, who was placed in a lock-down facility because she continued to run away from services to return to the streets, described as a typical coping skill for trafficking survivors. When asked, "Why do girls run from services?" She replied:

> It's a million-dollar question. I think they do it because they're not ready. They're comfortable … and I'm going to use terminology that they're comfortable with, so they're comfortable 'on the street,' which is what … especially what my one client calls it. If I call her a victim or that she was trafficked, she gets pissed! Because she was on the street, that's her terminology and I accept that. So that's her comfort zone. So if she is feeling uncomfortable or she's having therapy where she is having to really focus on what happened to her, she will take off. If she is feeling like she isn't being heard by the therapist, by the staff in the residential facility, she will take off. I advocated for some home passes over the holidays, and she took off while on a home pass. And she said it was just too much, that was her description. And again, it's not for the specific drugs, she is not going out there to do drugs. She's not going out there to have sex, she's not going out there knowing any of this stuff, she just … that's where she feel comfortable and that's home to her.

This example illustrates several important things. First, victims do not always see themselves as victims. Second, the "fight or flight" action typical of those who experience trauma was not addressed in the setting she was in, suggesting sex-trafficking-specific, trauma-informed services are important. Third, she needed to feel like she was being listened to. There is a wealth of literature related to survivor-centered practices and improved outcomes in the domestic violence literature, and this may be a promising avenue for practices with sex trafficking survivors as well

(Nichols, 2013, 2014; Goodman & Epstein, 2008; Bennett-Catteneo & Goodman, 2010; Kulkarni, Bell, & Rhodes, 2012). Fourth, she needed to be around people who understood her. This indicates that survivor-led services, and/or accessing services with other girls like her, may be a promising direction for service provision to trafficked individuals as well. In addition, being provided with services and expertise by those who understand and can advocate using the language the victim uses, and whose expertise is specific to understanding the unique dynamics of sex trafficking, was found to be imperative in treating and preventing returning to a sex trafficking situation. Similar dynamics have been uncovered in other sites, as described in Chapter Seven.

"People Like Us ..."

Further, accessing services surrounded by others who had been through the same experience was also noted as important. Another individual working with trafficked adolescents stated:

> I definitely think that we need more safe places for these girls and also people that are there that have maybe gone through that, and can identify, and show them a better way. Because sometimes they don't think that we understand; that we don't know what's going on, but I think it needs to be safe and secure. I think there needs to be more treatment, specific treatment.

For example, another social service provider who worked with girls stated:

> And with the girls that I've worked with, here in Missouri, who have survived trafficking they'll say, especially my gal at 'Peaceful Valley' right now, I just saw her yesterday, and got stuck in that hail storm! But she will verbalize ... I ran because I don't like it here and I'm not getting what I need, which is so true and she's so eloquent in talking about that, because she'll say you know the girls that I'm there with they're angry, they hit people, but they haven't been on the street. They're there for different reasons. So

she said group therapy works on anger management, but she'll say but they don't understand why I'm angry. It's not for those reasons that everyone else is here for. So, she's been ready to move to the Covering House for, well, whenever she first heard about it, she wanted to go. She is incredibly excited about going to that. The thought of going to a place that's just for 'people like her' who have been on the street, she is beyond excited about sharing experiences with other people at the Covering House. [At Peaceful Valley] no one knows why she is there. No one knows her past, and she's not comfortable sharing that ... So, yeah I think trafficking-specific services are completely necessary, and I'm glad to see more of them, and we need all that they can offer.

Placement in a setting with other survivors who have similar experiences, and therapeutic techniques to specifically address trauma associated with those experiences, may prevent girls from running from services and the risk of being re-trafficked. The outcomes are as of yet unknown in the St. Louis area, yet, such techniques have been successful elsewhere (e.g., GEMS, Magdalene House Nashville) and may offer promising directions for social service provision.

Further, social service providers working with adults leaving prostitution reported that having others in a therapeutic setting with a similar experience also helped to develop trust, feelings of safety, and a community of survivors among adult trafficking victims. Importantly, trust and relationship building were related to this model. One survivor stated:

Magdalene only works with women over 18, that is, we are a two-year full-service wrap-around service for the women. They get two years treatment, they get trauma care, they get sexual trauma [therapy]. They learn about their body, they learn to love themselves. They spend the first four to six months just learning to heal. And get clean, get emotionally stable, get medically stable, and be able to build that trust. Of course then we go into.... it's a two-year program ... it's absolutely free. We can have up to eight [women in the program]. Our first home will take up to eight. And we want to the women to learn how to be in a community and be accountable for each other, and their journey. Be able to learn to hold each other account-able, and it's a sisterhood, because once you graduate ... we're a replica of the Magdalene National Program and that program went on for 17 years. And they have, two and a half years after graduation, they have a 76% success rate, that's just unheard of. We're talking about women who have worked their way up ...

The "sisterhood" or community of survivors was described as key to recovery. In addition to other participants in the program having similar experiences, it was also found that programmatic design, leadership, and practice involving formerly trafficked peo-ple was a promising path, detailed below.

In sum, non-sex-trafficking-specific services were described as ineffective, and resulted in girls running way from services and going back to what they knew. There appeared to be a near con-sensus among respondents when asked about services for sex traf-ficking survivors—such services needed to be trauma informed, provided by someone with expertise in that area, and in a setting inclusive of a community of survivors.

Survivor-Informed Programming

Another common theme addressed by respondents was the sup-port for survivor-led or survivor-informed programing. Several re-spondents noted that this style of programming was beneficial in that it provided mentorship and understanding from people who had experienced what the survivors had experienced. A survivor illustrated:

> ... if you have a survivor-led organization then you're al-ready creating a community of survivors. And it's not a community of survivors created and led by a well-meaning

social worker or somebody, it's created and led by a survivor. I think that ... it's possible that that's really really important. I think that ... sex trafficking trauma ... hits a sort of moral injury as people are forced to do things that they really don't want do ... awful things with strange men that you don't like, societal norms violated during the trauma repeatedly, repeatedly, repeatedly, often, so ... 'I was there, I know what it was like, I know why you had to do that' ... The community understands and there is a subculture the trafficker will create, there's a different language, everybody outside of the subculture is a square, they will never understand, they're never going to understand.

Accordingly, community building, and social bonds related to common experiences and understandings may be important to recovery. Further, there are national organizations devoted to creating a community of survivors, and survivor led organizations. This network provides a public statement of support and unity for survivors simply in its existence.

... So, yeah, and plus, since now there are national networks, like the National Survivor Network, which is, I think, extremely important in doing a whole lot of really good work on policy and other levels, that survivor-led organizations may be hooked into a much larger network in a way that someone who is not a survivor wouldn't be able to be. So, there's a big possibility of a lot of feeling of really big net of support and possibility under those survivors who are lucky enough to be in a survivor-led organization ...

Even if organizations do not have the opportunity to have a survivor as a practicing member of the organization, survivors can be involved in programmatic design. The executive director of The Covering House described the benefit of having a survivor with professional expertise as an MSW involved in developing the programming for the Covering House:

Why it's important is she brought obviously the research component when she created the model for us. But she coupled that with her experiences of what she had gone through, what it took for her to go through her healing process, and I loved the fact that sometimes she would look at things and say, 'Yeah this looks great in theory, but it's not really going to work. Because I've been there, I've seen this, and this would ...' so what she created for us was based on evidence and research coupled with her experiences. So, it makes it just a very valuable model for us.

Accordingly, the model combined both expertise and personal experience to produce a program that was both evidence-based as well as survivor-informed. In having other survivors review the programming, a service provider from The Covering House noted that the reviews were met with accolades, remembering or recognizing steps or stages in treatment that each survivor experienced, although not necessarily in the same way or in the same order. Survivors recognized important areas of the programming as common and important in their own recovery.

> ... when we used her [survivor and MSW] therapeutic model, and then we talked to other survivors, the skeleton [of the programming] was good for all of the survivors we talked to, they're like, 'Yeah.' So how they reached those things might have been different, but they're like, 'Yeah, that was my stage, those were my steps.' They may not have been the complete same order, but all of those things were things that I had to work through and learn. And so, it gives us a lot of insight. Bringing them in [survivors] to work with the clients, there's an automatic trust that's developed there, a different type of understanding that allows them some freedom and offers them a different type of hope and a different kind of understanding. And it's reinforced. The therapy model that she developed for us is very relational-driven, so it's something that even if we weren't working with survivors you could still utilize it other places, but the theory behind it is all geared

towards, how do you address the trauma through building relationships, and how do you make people feel safe?

Notably, this survivor-informed programming in part revolved around the relationship between safety, trauma, and trust. Further, survivor-informed programming may be more likely to produce trust and bonds among survivors, who reported feeling less likely to be judged and more likely to be understood in such settings. One social service provider, who worked with children in the foster care system, described her work with a minor who was sex trafficked who continued to run from services, but had a different reaction when she learned survivors were involved in the organization where she was going to be placed:

> I think with any kind of survivor services, whether it's sexual assault advocacy or domestic violence, I feel that the movement is so much more passionate when survivors are a part of it. As far as, the gal at 'Peaceful Valley' [sex-trafficked client], she was very excited about this whole thing [going to The Covering House]. And then, when she heard that survivors had been a part of the planning process, she was elated. She was sooo excited! She was like, 'Oh, they know!' And she kept saying, 'They know! They know!' So that was her description of it.

In fact, the involvement of survivors in the organizations was thought by many to reduce the likelihood of girls running from services. A social services provider described the importance of survivor-informed organizations in preventing girls leaving services:

> I believe if they were to speak to someone who has been through it themselves, that would ease up a lot of those peripheral behavior issues ... it just goes back to kids ... the stranger talk and stuff like trafficking and being sexually violated and power/control are really tough things for anybody to talk about, let alone kids that already have other forms of trauma in their life. So they see someone as a peer, and not necessarily as an authority figure, I

think that would make them much more prone to speak
up and to seek services and things like that....

Further, another survivor noted that survivor-informed organizations were important in the eyes of survivors, who may fear
judgment or feel like they may not be understood by service
providers who had not experienced what they had:

> Victims/survivors are not going to relate to somebody
> who is in any way judgmental or even doesn't understand
> the issue. And of course, it's kind of like when Amber
> Alert started developing focus groups and workshops that
> included the survivors of abduction, and parents of kids
> who had been abducted, like they worked really hard to
> have their program informed by those people who were
> actually impacted by the crime. And I just don't think that
> people coming in without firsthand knowledge of it are
> going to design programs that are ideal. They might be
> good, but input from a survivor is going to help make that
> program avoid the pitfalls that could happen without sur-
> vivor informed services and ... it's such a hard thing to
> describe. I think there are just a lot of things that people
> don't think about, that's been my experience is that there's
> a whole lot of things that people don't think about that a
> survivor of the crime will think about. And if someone
> has gotten to the point where they can actually, you know,
> engage in advocacy and program development around
> this issue, then likely, they have a whole lot of wisdom and
> knowledge that can be put into it. But what we think, so
> far, just anecdotally and looking around at the results of
> the organizations report those that are survivor-led appear
> to have better outcomes, again, we don't know for sure.
> It's looking that way. And I certainly know from my first-
> hand experience in working with survivor informed or
> survivor led or not survivor led organizations, that the re-
> sponse of the clientele, of the consumers of the services,
> really, really positive when they know that a survivor is at
> the helm, really positive, because they know that that per-

son understands what they've been through. They can relate.... Yeah ... like when I spent the summer at GEMS in
New York, Girls Educational Mentoring Services, like one
young woman said that GEMS is the only place where like
she can just relax. Literally she's on her guard every place
else. And another girl told me that it's one of the only
places where people don't look at her and say, 'Yeah,
there's a prostitute.' And these are girls who came into
GEMS like when they were like 13, 14, 15 years old.

Another survivor provided a similar response:

One thing is that it takes really specialized training to understand the problem, and kids who've been in this situation, or even adults who have been in this kind of situation, really are not going to trust and relate to someone
who doesn't 'get it' especially because as with any sex
crime there's ... there can be so much feelings of shame,
and of course, that's going to led to protecting one's self,
and defending one's self. Plus, it's such a complex trauma,
usually, that I mean, really if someone doesn't know what
they're doing when they're working with a victim of sex
trafficking, they are probably very likely going to get a lot
of dissociative responses. So that could be complete shut-
down, or hyper-activation, anger, defensiveness. It's just
really easy to do a lot more harm than good, and not get
anywhere at all, if people aren't trained when they're
working with this population.

One social service provider, the Director of Magdalene House,
noted that survivor involvement in organizations is not only important in the work with clients, but also with community members:

I just hired Christine McDonald [survivor], about a
month ago, as Director of Outreach and Advocacy for
Magdalene. She's been doing that kind of work for a long
time, and she was on our board, and I absolutely feel that
their voice is needed to be heard at every table. Whether
it's in a program like my own, whether it's informing law

enforcement and judges and others about that perspective, it's extremely important. I think when you hear firsthand stories like Christine's or Katie Rhodes, or all of the stories I've heard from women in Nashville who've gone through the Magdalene program there, when you hear their firsthand stories it changes your perception of what this issue looks like in our community.

In sum, training in sex-trafficking-specific, trauma-informed therapeutic practices was depicted as necessary by multiple respondents, but survivors additionally needed to be understood by people who had a similar experience. This could include someone they could relate to, such as a survivor-leader, or others in the program who had experienced trafficking. Those who are prostituted or sell sex are stigmatized in society; survivors may benefit from the support they can offer one another. They can talk to a social worker, but they may not feel like they can be totally open. Further, trust building is so important to trauma recovery, and one is more likely to build trust with someone who is like them and knows what they've been through. As a cautionary measure, the data presented in this section is limited. In depth evaluation of programmatic outcomes had not yet been conducted. Yet the perspectives and experiences of survivors and service providers can be viewed, while perhaps not as confirmed best practices, as promising directions for practice. Further, there is research evidence to support these claims, albeit in the areas of intimate partner violence, sexual assault, or trauma-based research. In addition to survivor informed programming building trust and feelings of acceptance, survivor-defined practices was also found to be beneficial to survivors, particularly as a means toward empowerment and recovery.

Survivor-Defined Practices

An overarching program addressing trust, trauma, and safety was thought to be potentially important for treatment and empowerment. At the same time, within this specialized programming, tailoring services to specific needs was also emphasized as a promising avenue of practice. A social service provider with The Covering House illustrated how individually tailored services were also important, within services specifically designed for sex trafficking survivors:

> ... when we were talking to the different survivors as we were going through the therapy model, there was this kind of skeleton [overarching program] that we went through that was similar for all of them. Like initially they all had to feel safe, [but] how they got that safety looks different. When a girl comes in, we ask them, 'What do you need to feel safe?' And then they share that with the group, because that could look very different for me, I might need you to give me five minutes to just be quiet when I'm upset. Another girl might need to be able to step out of the room, there's a different level of safety. The safety is the same, that's the same for everyone, they need to feel safe, but how they get there looks different.

While feeling safe was an important part of programmatic design, it is important to note that what one individual needed to feel safe was distinct from what another would need. The programming at the Covering House was described as individualized, within an overarching program.

In addition to safety, personal empowerment (e.g., agency) was also a part of programming at The Covering House, and also at Magdalene House. This was described in terms of self-efficacy by one social service provider at The Covering House. Self-efficacy was included as a part of the overarching programming at the Covering House, but the way to this empowerment was different for each girl. A social service provider delineated:

> Yeah, we focus a lot on the word self-efficacy because we just it kind of related to what do you see about yourself, that internal, like where do you get that worth internally. So we focus a lot on that. We focus a lot on what are your controlling images whether it's from what people have told you, whether it's the media. Some girls look at mag-

azines and it's not going to affect their view of themselves, but some girls it does. Other girls, it might be their boyfriend that controls it while another girl might be completely confident in that. And so helping them realize what their controlling images are, helping them see what their truth worth is. A lot of our programming is not as much focused on let's talk about your trauma, it's focused on that with the idea of that leading us into the trauma and focus so that they have a healthy place to come to, and how that develops ... What is appropriate for each girl? What do they need in order to have that worth? What is their worth kind of come from or stem from?

In addition to developing healthy images of self-worth as a means to empowerment, the programming also included developing an interest. This was intended as a form of sensory therapy. Yet developing or cultivating an interest may also relate to the empowerment of survivors as well. Girls can choose an interest to build upon and develop. They are able to control what they do in the context of this interest. This may include gardening, cooking, art, or other interests. Exhibiting control over something in a healthy way is important in addressing trauma. The idea is that the survivor could not control what happened to them, but they can control an interest, this may build into feeling control over other aspects of their lives as well. Controlling one's own decisions and outcomes is key to developing empowerment, supported by decades of research examining intimate partner violence (see Nichols, 2014; Goodman & Epstein, 2008).

Empowerment can be facilitated by the practices of social service providers, as well as programmatic design. A social service provider from The Covering House stated:

And that's the whole ... like when we're training our staff we talk about, you know, initially we may have to set boundaries for them, or we may have to advocate for them, but we may have to help them regulate their behaviors. But the goal is to do that for themselves. Eventually I want them to be their own advocates. I want them to be able to regulate themselves. I want them to be able to say this is what my boundaries are, and this is how I can do it and have that empowerment to do it, with support from us. So it changes from us having to do it for them, to you have a voice, now you have a choice. Like we've talked to some of our adult survivors I work with and one of them said just a few weeks ago she's like it was hard for me to even process past peanut and jelly, because I had to learn how to make my choices. So, we may have to help them initially make that choice, of this is what dinner is right now. But next week what do you want? And do you want to learn how to cook that meal? So you can make it for yourself when you leave? So that's an empowering thing. Not just a ... it gives them kind of control over things in a healthy way.

A survivor and board member of The Magdalene House, providing services for adults, also related the program to meeting the individual needs of women, and supporting their ability to make their own choices and control their own lives:

We believe that they should be allowed the privilege of finding their own way and encourage what that ... should look like. People have decided when they could eat, when they could sleep, where they live, who they sleep with, and we feel that it's honorable to a human being to be allowed the opportunity to identify who they are.

Similarly, the director of operations at The Covering House noted that survivors' experiences with trafficking should not define who they are, and it was important to note girls' individual personalities, characteristics, goals, and skills. Consequently, focusing on the needs, interests, and goals of each survivor within the overarching program of sex-trafficking-specific services may work to facilitate empowerment and agency of each individual survivor. While the outcomes of this design have not been widely evaluated in the context of sex trafficking, decades of research examining domestic violence victims and empowerment finds that when survivors have control of their own situations, and services are tailored to individual needs and choices, the outcomes are significantly improved (see Nichols, 2014; Goodman & Epstein, 2008). Accordingly, this may be a promising direction for practice with sex trafficking survivors. In addition to navigating effective and ineffective practices, social service providers, survivors, and those in the justice system noted gaps in available services that also presented challenges.

Gaps in Services

Lack of Shelter Space

Respondents noted that available shelter or housing was lacking for girls, boys, adults, and LGBTQ individuals. Once sex-trafficked or sexually exploited survivors were identified, social service providers often faced challenges in finding a place to send them. One social service provider who worked with homeless youth stated, "We can find boys and girls all day long who want help, but I have nowhere to send them." When asked if St. Louis had enough shelter space available for sex-trafficked or commercially sexually exploited people, another social service provider who also worked with homeless youth similarly indicated:

> No. No we don't, and like I'm not one that likes to work from scarcity mindset, but the truth of the matter is that, you know, especially in the winter, it's easier in the warmer months, but especially in the winter, like we struggle with having enough beds, and I think we could probably have 10 or 12 more shelters and we would still have youth that need placement options …

The Covering House is one of relatively few shelters nationwide, 38 in all, who provide explicitly for survivors of sex trafficking or commercial sexual exploitation under the age of 18. At the time of the writing of this book, the organization was just opening their house, after providing direct outpatient services for years. The social service providers of this organization indicated that the demand for this type of housing exceeded the number of beds they had available. The executive director of the Covering House described this need:

> Yeah there is a huge need. We're about ready to open with about 8 beds, and we have [them] already waiting or have contacted us. And we know that we will fill up maybe within a week. Magdalene House, who's going to be opening up, their goal is sometime this summer and they're going to be working with 18-and-over-year-olds. And they're going to have 7 beds. So, and theirs is a two-year program, ours is a one-year program, and so, you could have almost a shelter on every block and still not meet the need that's happening.

Several respondents outside of the shelter system also noted that trafficking victims could be identified, but there was nowhere for them to go. In fact, lack of shelter space for sex-trafficked people was indicated as one of the most pressing issues in terms of lack of services in the St. Louis bi-state area.

Lack of Services for Adult Women

In addition to the limited space for those in need of shelter more generally, specifically, housing specifically for adult women who had been trafficked or were otherwise leaving the life of prostitution was extremely limited, not just in St. Louis, but in the entire nation. The Magdalene house, serving adult women leaving prostitution, was in the process of opening at the time of the writing of this book, with just seven beds. The director of the Magdalene house indicated a high level of demand for services:

> But the demand for service I don't know how to explain it.... when we're getting phone calls every single day ... we're getting phone calls from people who are local, we're getting calls from people out-of-state wondering when our house is going to be open. They've read about Nashville ... we'll be the third city that has Magdalene program up and running ... the demand is significant.

And this is coming from women who know what the program is … understand what it is that they have to do to be a part of that. And it's daunting.

Based upon the number of phone calls the Magdalene House was getting, and the demand for their services, it was clear that there were not enough services to meet the needs of the women that needed and wanted them. When asked about the demand for their program, and if she thought that there were enough programs to meet the demand, the director of the organization responded:

> No. Not even close. It's not even close, we're not even close, to having the kinds and number of services we need to really effect some change. They [the community] are starting to care. And I hope that leads to more investment in the kind of help these women need. You would like to think so, but that often sort of lags behind the change of attitude and by that point you've already missed a lot of women that could end up dead on the street.

The organization was privately funded, and consequently relied on community awareness and related contributions. A survivor and member of the Magdalene house pointed out that people have to care about those who have been involved in prostitution in order for those who wanted help to be able to access it. She indicated a lack of public and political support for adults who experienced trafficking or were otherwise leaving prostitution:

> We need services for pre-movement [anti-trafficking movement] survivors, which are, women that exited before there was anybody even willing to talk about it. There's no services, there's no funding, there's no nothing if you're a pre-movement survivor. And if you're over 18, there's nothing! There's nothing! Because once you turn 18 you're a criminal.

Importantly, this survivor noted that services for adult women were scarce, and adults were also more likely to be viewed as criminals rather than as people who wanted and deserved assistance. She elaborated to describe the program's funding streams, "We don't take government money because they're not going to give it to us." Importantly, she described how government funding was not earmarked for services to adult survivors of sex trafficking or those leaving prostitution. This indicates that adults involved in prostitution are marginalized not only in the community, but through funding streams as well.

At the same time, respondents noted that there was a push in the anti-trafficking community to make changes in the justice system in terms of arrest and sentencing of prostitutes. Work in this area involved attempting to stop arresting adults who sold sex, and to reduce the charge from a felony to a misdemeanor on the Missouri side (this was already accomplished on the Illinois side). Several respondents highlighted that the felony record prevented women from leaving prostitution who wanted to, as it became difficult to gain legitimate employment with a felony prostitution record. Moreover, steep fines also more or less ensured continued prostitution as a way of paying off the fine (see Chapter Three). One respondent noted associated challenges, in that there was nowhere to refer women when they sought social services or encountered the justice system:

> The problem, I think, that we all face when we're looking at that system is that okay so if they stop arresting women, where do they refer them to? So it's a really stupid cycle that we're in right now. And that is something that we hear from the judges all of the time, we don't want to put her back in jail. Where do we put her?

This example illustrates both paternalism in "putting" her somewhere, as well as the fact that there aren't enough adequate services available. Most domestic violence shelters do not accept prostituted individuals, unless domestic violence was also present. Moreover, with a felony prostitution charge, such women would be excluded from many shelters. Women were identified who wanted assistance, but there were very few options available.

Lack of Shelter for Men and Boys

Respondents noted that a general lack of available services to meet the demand for such services was the largest gap in addressing trafficking in the St. Louis area. Further, services and shelter explicitly for trafficked boys were found to be virtually absent in the St. Louis area. For example, one social service provider stated, "I would say probably the biggest gap right now would be services, and then, services for boys in general. There is nothing in the area for boys." There were shelters that boys could access, and various drop-in and outreach services that provided for boys, but not specifically for sex-trafficked boys. As discussed above, such services may be necessary to address the complex trauma that sex-trafficked individuals experience. A respondent working in the Juvenile Division of the Family Courts agreed, "And we've had calls. And we've been able to try to find them resources but even the resources are few for boys, very few." He estimated that about ten percent of the kids he encountered who had been trafficked were boys, ninety percent were girls. The director of Rescue and Restore, as well as several other social service providers who worked with homeless youth, in foster care, domestic violence outreach programs, or outreach programs for troubled youth indicated that there was a lack of space for boys who had been sex-trafficked:

> We don't have enough beds, which there are not enough places to put victims. 'Jaden' was exactly right, we do these outreach things so we can increase identification, and then they call, and we have nowhere to take them. And then tied to that, we have no dedicated shelters for male human trafficking victims, none! They almost don't get any media press, and sometimes they're mentioned like as an afterthought: 'Oh, yes, and by the way, boys are also victims.'

There were shelters for boys in St. Louis, but none specifically dedicated to those who had been sex trafficked or commercially sexually exploited. Yet it was found that there was in fact demand for shelter services for sex trafficked boys and young men in St. Louis, who were primarily engaging in the "survival sex" form of sex trafficking or sexual exploitation (see Chapter Three). Further, another social service provider stated that there was just one shelter in the nation that specifically provided services to sex-trafficked boys:

> .... It's a little bit more hidden, but almost every presentation I go to or every time I talk to social service providers the number 1 question is: Do you have services for boys? So I think we're seeing more and more cases for whatever reason it is just a little less talked about. There's not a lot of homes. So I think the last time we checked there were, I don't know, I think there was a home opening up in North Carolina that was the first home, home, like there are only like 12 to 15 beds available for boys across the nation.

In addition, the non-sex-trafficking-specific shelters that were available were described as problematic. One respondent who worked in mental health stated:

> I think always you could use more. I think the areas where I feel I see the most need are probably around housing programs. And because the men ... if you're over 18 and especially if you're over 20 and you're homeless the shelter options or other programs and things are not good, like I have a lot of people that I've talked to ... if your choice is like go to Larry Rice [homeless shelter] or sleep like in a ditch somewhere, I mean, a lot of people would prefer to not go to some of the shelters.

For men and boys who experienced sex trafficking or exploitation, shelter and housing options were limited. The available shelters or spaces were not viewed as desirable because of overt drug use outside the shelter, harassment by other residents, and theft. This shelter was also one of the few options available to LGBTQ individuals over the age of 18 as well.

Lack of Shelter for LGBTQ Individuals

As described previously, LGBTQ individuals were at a higher risk of sex trafficking in the form of "survival sex," which was interrelated with runaway or throwaway status and consequent homelessness. Shelter specifically for sex-trafficked or commercially sexually exploited LGBTQ youth was also described as a gap in services in the St. Louis area. One program director stated:

> Ours [program] is designed for girls 13 to 17, but if coming into the program, she's lesbian, we don't distinguish one way or the other. I mean we welcome them. The [issue with accepting] transgender [girls] is a little more sensitive in that we could provide out-client services for them, in fact, we've talked about that. To do that legally through the state of Missouri, we would have to have them in under their physiological gender [e.g., the gender assigned to them at birth] and not how they identify, which can be awkward and confusing, so we're not set up for something like that, with just 8 beds. But there is going to be a need for that as well, absolutely!

This social service provider indicated limitations imposed by the state related to admitting trans-girls into their program. There were no sex-trafficking-specific shelters for trans-people, as well as gay males, who were trafficked or commercially sexually exploited in the St. Louis bi-state area. There was a Youth in Need shelter for youth and a homeless shelter for adults that were among the few available options. Respondents indicated that homeless shelters in St. Louis were often unsafe, people used drugs right outside the Center, their money was stolen, and people were sometimes harassed by other shelter residents. When asked about this, one respondent working in mental health stated:

> That's probably New Life Evangelistic Center ... yeah ... which is Larry Rice's program downtown. And there's actually.... this is probably not.... there's rumors about all kinds of stuff that happens down there. So, I mean certainly there is some stuff that happens down there, and I don't think that the agency can necessarily be blamed for it all, but there's a lot of stuff happening there and not enough oversight of it.

Consequently, some survivors viewed selling sex for a place to stay (e.g., survival sex) or staying on the streets as preferable to staying in some of the homeless shelters. As a result, LGBTQ individuals were at a heightened risk of engaging in sex trafficking or commercial sexual exploitation in the form of survival sex, in part due to lack of shelter options.

Lack of LGBTQ-Specific Services

A significant problem identified in the St. Louis area was not only lack of shelter for LGBTQ youth, but lack of culturally competent services more generally. Respondents described not only a lack of understanding of LGBTQ people, but direct discrimination as well. The respondents also noted that LGBT individuals may experience unique forms of trauma requiring specific expertise in addressing that trauma. This included bullying or ostracization from their schools and in street life, in addition to rejection from their parents. Consequently, the need for culturally competent trauma-informed services was demarcated as extremely important to the recovery of LGBTQ youth. Revictimization in being further traumatized by culturally incompetent staff could potentially pose as a barrier to future use of services and accessing help.

Respondents indicated LGBTQ individuals may experience unique trauma related to their sex trafficking experience. For example, rejection from their families and schools, and consequent runaway or throwaway status directly associated with their sexual orientation was specific to LGBTQ youth. One sex trafficking survivor, a gay man who experienced CSEC in his youth, noted:

> I'll share, like, from myself ... I was in a Youth-In-Need shelter and I was staying there at the time, because I was kicked out, my mom kicked me out. I came from a violent family already. I had many layers of generations of violence, and then, my high school at the time which was private Jesuit hall Catholic High School kicked me out as well, so I kind of lost my family and sort of my school community support ... I was suicidal I tried to kill myself, and then, I was placed in the Youth-In-Need shelter after having actually been homeless and couch surfing for a bit.

The experience of rejection on multiple fronts, leading to a sex trafficking situation due to others' reactions to their sexual orientation, makes the experience unique, requiring services tailored toward understanding this rejection and background, and the way it is interconnected with sexual exploitation. While opposite-sex attracted individuals also were often runaways or rejected by their parents, and also came from abusive homes, this rejection was not specifically directed toward their sexual orientation, suggesting survivor-centered therapy inclusive of this unique trauma may be needed.

In addition to parental and school rejection, some social service providers described working with LGBTQ youth who had been trafficked or exploited as a way of "turning them back" from their sexual orientation. This sexual trauma, specifically targeting their sexual orientation, was also unique to LGBTQ people. For example, when asked what was missing, or still needed in St. Louis, one social service provider stated:

> ... Having highly culturally competent and inclusive agencies, because, if they're [LGBTQ youth] already on the streets they have already been ostracized in some way. The likelihood that they've experienced bullying or someone ... a lot of times we see kids who have been exploited trying to make them into a man, or make them into a real girl so that they can turn them back, or something like that, you know, some of these really horrible beliefs that are out there. And so, they have a unique type of trauma that is different than a youth who is not engaged in same sex relationships might experience.

This social service provider noted that LGBTQ youth held unique experiences based upon their gender identity or sexual orientation. It is important that social service providers are familiar with the possibility of these distinct experiences, and that victimization may be heightened for LGBTQ youth, so they can provide for these specific needs/trauma accordingly in practice. One social service provider described what she meant by "culturally competent services" in her statement: "Going back to the LGBTQ kiddos, I think having more places that are open and affirming, welcoming, and inclusive for them would be awesome." She indicated that things such as gender-inclusive language and embracing the ways people self-identify in shelters was important:

> ... I think that having services that really meet their unique experiences and needs in order for them to heal and grow and be able to be fully functioning citizens in the world ... having just like gender inclusive language that we use with our kids. And if you.... a lot of things shelters [in other areas] are doing is if you identify as male, regardless of your biology, you get to stay on the male side of the shelter, and things like that. Just so that they are not internalizing any more discrimination that they have already experienced, I think is that it's just going to be an extra burden that they're carrying as they try to move forward.

Another social service provider and survivor described how his organization, which provided a myriad of services related to domestic and sexual violence, moved toward inclusive language as an expression of cultural competency:

> So here, for instance, at Outreach to Safety, we serve adult women who are survivors of domestic, partner and sexual violence. When I was hired I remember them telling me that. And they said, 'We serve adult women, or we serve women who are survivors of domestic, partner or sexual violence.' 'We serve teens, boys and girls ... we serve boys and girls and we serve women.' And I said okay. So, I'm going to start asking some questions, like, so, when you say teens, boys and girls, would you see trans? They're like, 'Yeah, of course.' And I was like, so why don't we say all genders? We see teens of all genders. And then, when we say women who do you mean? 'We mean women.' And I was like, would you see trans women? And they're like, 'If she identifies as a woman so that's a trans woman, so yeah.' And I was like, I want you to say that explicitly. So

as opposed to, 'We see women.' I would love it if we said, 'We see adult women, that includes cisgender women, we see trans women.' Even for like our marketingness this June for Pride I was like, let's let that be one of our campaigns is that we say that loud and proud and that is what we're saying at our table. Because if you're a trans woman—who, inherently trans women of color deal with the highest rates of violence—you are not going to think, 'Oh, these mainstream second-wave feminist organizations I can come into and feel safe and included.' You're going to come in being like, 'No, actually, like, I've had the door shut in my face so many times, why would I think that this would be a place for me?'

Importantly, providing culturally competent services is important in practice, as individuals who do not receive adequate services that are welcoming and affirming are more likely to be revictimized by returning to harmful environments when they are not accepted or do not feel services are inclusive of their identity or sexual orientation. Another social service provider noted that the failure rate of services for LGBTQ youth was likely to be much higher if social service providers were not able to relate to or address LGBTQ survivors in a culturally competent way:

I think that's absolutely imperative because otherwise we're going to have people coming into our doors that we don't even know what's going on. So, if we don't know what's going on we're not going to be able to address it. And then, the likelihood that we're going to have pretty high recidivism rates right back to the street or right back to the exploitation of the situation is pretty high, if we don't know as a social service provider what we're doing.

Significantly, this statement reveals that if one is not aware of specific trauma, or even how to engage with someone in a culturally competent way, they are not able to specifically tailor practice towards that trauma, or to even recognize the anticipation of discrimination and non-acceptance.

In addition to lack of culturally competent services and knowledge of unique trauma, discrimination within social services was also identified by multiple respondents. Two social service providers even stated that the work they did with LGBTQ youth and issues itself was viewed as controversial. "I think it's just because like … if people were to … I know that the work that I do is very controversial on some people's eyes, especially my work with transgender clients and stuff." Some social service providers who worked with LGBTQ people described a general stigma in society, and even among some practitioners in social services. Another respondent, who largely worked with people 18–24, including LGBTQ individuals stated:

> Even in the social service world. There's a lot of people who are really, I think mostly not aware but also have strong negative reactions once they hear a little bit, and I think it takes them awhile of really having long conversations about why are we doing what we're doing, before people kind of might not be alarmed, I don't know why it's so controversial but it sure seems like it is sometimes.

Two social service providers indicated having issues with a couple of organizations in terms of acceptance and understanding the needs of LGBTQ clients:

> Also there is some conservative evangelical organizations and folks who are really interested in sex trafficking, but their vision of what they think that looks like … I think that we tried to kind of build some connections with them, but I think that we were really alarmed and concerned by some of the stuff they were saying about LGBT people. Like one of the people that came from their agency made some comments about how some people become LGBT because of sex work and sort of implying that, I can't even remember all of the stuff that she said, but there were some things … and also just some of the basic LGBT terminology, I was like, I don't think that's a safe place for LGBT people.

When asked what he meant by "not safe," he replied:

> When I say 'not safe' I just mean that I think they have good intentions but I don't think that they even have a basic understanding about like, what's the difference between sexual orientation and gender identity. And like, there was like, and we had conversations about like, will you accept transgender clients? And they, I think, they were focusing on women, and so it's was like, will you accept transgender women in your program? And they really made it seem like that was not something they were comfortable with and that's probably actually for the best, because the best place is with people who understood them.

Thus, available services were viewed by some respondents, not as a potential safe haven and space for recovery and services, but as a site of revictimization and further harm. If LGBTQ people encounter discrimination and non-acceptance in social services, they are more likely to return to the streets and to be retrafficked. This revolving door implicates ineffective social service provision due to cultural incompetency as an area in need of change to avoid retrafficking of LGBTQ people. In addition, the need for service providers who are culturally competent, or who are themselves LGBTQ identified may be an important direction for service provision. Another social service provider, who was also a survivor, indicated experiencing overt discrimination toward LGBTQ people:

> I cannot tell you how many times I go and talk to adults and there are actively people who will share with me at the time, 'Oh, yeah, we have half our staff not come to this because they said their religion wouldn't allow them to.' I mean that's the culture that we exist in. So, I show up and I'm like okay, you know ... and there are professional organizations whether it's a school district, whether it's a residential treatment center, whether it's a place like Covenant House, Mary Grove, Lakeside. There are staff

members who are active, actively resistantly homophobic. So, if you have staff members modeling that behavior, right, how the hell are they going to keep that young person or those young people that they have who are there safe? And the fact that the staff doesn't hold them accountable, so the staff says, well, you know, it doesn't go with their religion. And I'm like, there is no excuse for that. And I'm like, if you're a youth service provider, if you're an advocate for young people, at the end of the day, your job is to keep that young person safe and help them feel ... help them tap into resources. Hopefully you're doing some sort of positive youth development, you're also making them feel empowered. Like those are what I call the tenets of what you have, as an adult who is a provider for youth. I find that there's still this kind of like, no, we don't really need all of our staff to come down on this or protect all youth.

In addition to not getting the care they needed, LGBTQ youth may also be exposed to some homophobic or transphobic service providers. One survivor and social service provider illustrated:

A lot of service providers in St. Louis are really homophobic and transphobic, still. And a lot of people who do service-providing work, and I've realized this, having recently done this position in the past year, a lot of people who specifically work with these like youth at risk who are most vulnerable, a lot of them come into it because of their religious calling. So you have people come in like well, Jesus, God Allah or whoever, right?, says I'm doing this work to save the people or to save the young ones, and this is a part of my work at being a good religious or Christian or whatever your faith is, and those same reasons are given because now I don't have to advocate for this LGBT community. And it's like no, no, no, you don't get to pick and choose. And it's allowed.

Yet another social service provider indicated that sexual orientation, gender identity, and race intersected to impact the experiences of sex-trafficked people:

> We're not taking care of our young people. We're doing kind of a shitty job, and like really protect them. And LGBTQ youth specifically, and, let's get more specific, LGBTQ youth of color, LGBTQ youth of color who are, a lot of them are gender non-conforming or trans, right, like these youth are disenfranchised. These youth have people really shitting on them, and we need to do something about it. And we don't have that.

Respondents indicated some social service providers, particularly in children's services, were identified as being overtly homophobic and transphobic. Yet their job was to advocate for all children, regardless of sexual orientation or gender identification. This form of institutional discrimination directed toward LGBTQ youth was identified as a barrier to accessing services by four out of thirty-one the respondents in this study, by two cis/straight social service providers and two gay-identified social service providers.

Further, another institutional barrier that may disproportionately affect LGBTQ youth is the need for some shelters to have parental consent to stay in the shelter. One survivor noted this as problematic in terms of LGBTQ youth accessing shelter:

> Also, to enter into a youth shelter back in the day, and this is still the case, your parent has to sign you in. So, how crazy is that? Your parent is kicking you out because they don't want you in the house for being gay because they [don't] approve of your lifestyle, whatever, the BS reason is they give, and then, you're supposed to say, 'Hey Mom/Dad, Grandma/Grandpa, by the way, can you go sign me into the shelter?' Most of the times they're going to say 'No! Fuck you! You're gone!'

Institutional discrimination from some individuals in children's services, problematic shelter entrance requirements, lack of shelter, and rejection from family members conflate to produce few choices for LGBTQ youth. This increases the likelihood of returning to the streets and engaging in survival sex, identified as a common form of sex trafficking in the St. Louis area.

Chapter Summary

In sum, various organizations in the St. Louis bi-state area worked to provide direct services to sex trafficking survivors, and offered insights into promising directions in both programmatic design and social work practices. Those in the social service and justice system sectors described challenges with available resources. Specifically, lack of shelter space and sex-trafficking-specific services were delineated as problematic, in addition to lack of culturally competent services addressing LGBTQ trafficked people. Non-sex-trafficking-specific services often failed survivors. Juvenile detention centers, foster care placements, rehabilitation centers, mental hospitals, and domestic violence services were described as ineffective, often leading to the revolving door back into street life. Survivors and those experienced in working with sex trafficking survivors highlighted the need for sex-trafficking-specific services and trauma-informed care to address the unique trauma of sex trafficking victims. Further, programs involving a community of survivors, as well as survivor-informed and survivor-defined services that worked to facilitate empowerment/agency and to build trust were described as encouraging avenues for practice.

Chapter 7

Implications

Throughout this book, we have addressed the issues of sex and labor trafficking evident in St. Louis, Missouri and the bi-state area. We focused on victim characteristics, vulnerabilities, migration patterns, and the various forms of exploitation. Additionally, we discussed the efforts made by various actors involved in anti-trafficking endeavors. Specifically, we focused our attention on social service providers and actors in the legal arena. We not only analyzed these groups separately, but we also stressed the importance of collaboration. That being said, the attention now must turn to what can be done to better the anti-trafficking efforts, not just in St. Louis and the bi-state area, but throughout the country. The cases that we have examined in this book are not fringe cases. Human trafficking occurs in almost every corner of the United States. It may be hidden behind landscaped walls or embedded in Internet advertising. Boyfriends are selling their girlfriends at parties. Parents are selling their children for drugs. Runaways and throwaways are picked up by buyers and pimps, who are actively searching for vulnerable people to exploit. Undocumented immigrants are found working to pay off an endless debt in chicken factories or seasonal orchards. The victims and survivors are real, not just a representation of media sensationalism. Therefore, we believe that it is not only important to tell the stories we heard throughout our research, but also discuss the implications of our findings that can be valuable to all of those involved in anti-trafficking efforts, not just those in St. Louis and the bi-state area. Regions with similar contextual dynamics to those expressed in this book may benefit from modeling the successful anti-trafficking efforts illustrated throughout. This final chapter is divided into three sections: implications for social service providers, implications for law enforcement, and implications for policy. We conclude the chapter and the book by projecting the future of human trafficking and the anti-trafficking efforts in the United States.

Implications for Social Service Providers

Sex Trafficking

The research findings suggest a number of promising developments for social work practice with survivors of sex trafficking, including sex-trafficking-specific services, trauma-informed practice, survivor-informed or survivor-involved programming, and survivor defined practice. Yet these recommendations should be received with caution, as comprehensive evaluation has not yet been conducted with the sample of survivors and service providers whose perceptions were included in this book. Consequently, the recommendations provided here should not be viewed as confirmed "best practices." Rather, they should be viewed as promising directions for practice in need of further research. While recognizing the limitations of yet-to-be evaluated programmatic design, it should be noted that the recommendations drawn from the respondents in this study are evidence-based in other areas of study, such as domestic violence, sexual assault, and trauma-care or in organizations working with trafficked people or women leaving prostitution located in other sites. This is likely why such techniques were incorporated into practice and programming in the first place. Further, the expertise of those who work directly with survivors, as well as survivors themselves, should be valued in the same way other experts are valued, such as doctors who work directly with patients.

First, the inclusion of survivor leadership or participation into programmatic design is supported by other work examining women leaving prostitution (Lloyd, 2012; Oselin, 2014). This work finds that survivor mentorship, and a community of survivors, benefits recovery from prostitution. For example, GEMS, an organization serving prostituted girls, uses a survivor-leadership and mentorship model, and boasts a nearly 75% success rate of girls leaving prostitution and moving on with their lives in positive empowering directions (GEMS, 2014). Similarly, The Magdalene House Program, also referred to as the Nashville Model, as it began in Nashville, TN, serves adult women leaving prostitution, also shows success. The St. Louis branch was examined in this study. The program also uses a community of survivors as a part of its therapeutic model, and claims a 72% success rate of women who are free from drugs and prostitution two and a half years after beginning the program (Eden House, 2014). Similarly, Oselin (2014) examined four prostitute-serving organizations in Los Angeles, Hartford, Chicago, and Minneapolis, and found that a community of survivors and survivor mentorship was significantly important to recovery. Those who were in residential care, who had survivor mentorship, and support from other survivors who were also receiving care, had significantly better outcomes than those who were receiving outpatient care, and who didn't have mentorship and a community of survivors (Oselin, 2014). Thus, programmatic design inclusive of survivor mentorship and a community of survivors is supported by the research.

Further, a growing body of work finds support for survivor-defined practices, which work to facilitate empowerment of women by respecting their choices and decisions, and including them as active agents in their own recovery (Kulkarni, Bell, & Rhodes, 2012; Goodman & Epstein, 2008; Nichols, 2014; Bennett-Catteneo & Goodman, 2010; Bennett & Goodman, 2005; Zweig & Burt, 2007). Although much of this research is in the area of intimate partner violence, researchers find survivor-defined practices reduce the likelihood of future abuse, and are associated with lower levels of depression and higher levels of satisfaction with services. This model is also called the empowerment model, or woman-defined, woman-centered, person-centered, or survivor-centered practice, with empowerment serving as the focal point. When individuals make their own choices and guide their own destinies, they are empowered to continue this control of their own lives following treatment (Goodman & Epstein, 2008; Nichols, 2014). Similarly, this is a potentially promising practice in work with sex trafficking survivors, as trafficked people can be empowered by making their own choices and determining their own goals (Lloyd, 2012).

In addition, trauma-informed practice is supported by research examining the experiences of trauma survivors. Such practices may include therapeutic models such as eye movement desensitization and reprocessing, which has shown positive outcomes among sexual abuse survivors and individuals with PTSD (Jordan, 2010; Edmond, Sloan, & McCarty, 2004; Schubert & Lee, 2009). Further, cognitive behavioral therapy, or cognitive restructuring, has also shown positive outcomes among sexual abuse survivors, including adolescent girls (Foa, Hembree, Cahill, Rauch, Riggs, & Feeny, 2005; Foa, McLean, Capaldi, & Rosenfield, 2013; Galovski, Blain, Mott, Elwood, Houle, 2012; Rizvi, Vogt, & Resick, 2009). Moreover, trauma-based group therapy approaches are also shown to be effective (Mendelsohn, Herman, Schatzow, Coco, Kallivayalil, & Levitan, 2011; Fritch & Lynch, 2008). This research generally finds higher rates of successful recovery among trauma survivors experiencing trauma-informed therapy. Some forms of trauma-informed therapy work to develop understandings of and address "fight or flight" responses characteristic of trauma survivors. In the present study, this dynamic was associated with girls running from services, calling for trauma-informed care. Trauma-informed care for sex trafficking survivors is important, because the trauma sex-trafficked people experience is unique and multifaceted.

In addition to these promising practices, access to shelter or transitional housing was found to be important in this study. This would provide the necessary environment for the abovementioned practices to take place. Respondents noted the demand for such services far exceeded availability, and that they could find trafficking survivors all day long, but had nowhere to take them. In addition, respondents indicated long term follow up would benefit survivors. This is a little-explored area of research. Yet, successful programs, such as the Magdalene House, require two years of residential care and direct service. Similarly, Oselin (2014) found that women were much more likely to successfully transition out of prostitution with residential care and long-term follow up upon leaving residential care. She noted that organizations offering outpatient care had significantly lower levels of success in transitioning women out of prostitution. Thus, while the research pool in this area is currently small, there is a growing body of work finding support for long term residential services. Such services should also be specific to sex trafficking.

Sex-trafficking-specific services are important, because of the unique trauma that sex trafficking survivors experience. Further, non-sex-trafficking-specific services (e.g., juvenile detention, foster care) are problematic, as they are associated with re-trafficking and girls running away from services. Such environments often do not work to address the problem, do not offer a community of survivors with similar experiences or survivor mentorship, nor do they typically provide trauma-informed care. Sex-trafficking-specific services must also be LGBTQ inclusive, with practitioners educated in cultural competency and the unique trauma LGBTQ people are more likely to encounter in their trafficking experiences.

Social service provision is a way of responding to the problem, but it does not address it at its source. To prevent sex trafficking, dealing with larger issues such as poverty, cultural norms about sex and gender, and building stronger social institutions is necessary. Addressing issues with weak social institutions, such as poverty and problematic home lives, as well as broken education systems, increasing the minimum wage, expanding welfare and daycare subsidies and provisions for mental health and substance abuse is admittedly difficult, particularly in the political climate of the present day. At the same time, it should be noted that these are recognized risk factors, and bolstering social safety nets is recommended in order to ameliorate some of the risk factors associated with sex trafficking.

Labor Trafficking

Given the overall attention paid to sex trafficking, the research suggests that those in the social service sector need to begin broadening the scope of interest to include the identification and protection of victims of labor trafficking. Our findings indicated that many of those identified in various forms of labor trafficking were foreign nationals in search of a better life situation. Much of the recruitment strategies involved bait and switch; the promise of a standard paying job only to be told that the job did not exist once the migrant laborer was stranded. Once stranded, many migrant laborers were told to pay for a job placement up-front, already beginning work in a cycle of debt. Migrants moved with the agricultural season, and therefore, were difficult to identify. Those that had been identified quickly disappeared as the work moved to a new location.

Given what is known about those migrant laborers, it is necessary for social service providers to allocate more resources and time to the agricultural sector. Social service providers need to coordinate a system of support that is unique to those victims of labor trafficking. Given the general language barriers, there needs to be an increase in translating agencies throughout the region as well as training in English proficiency. Housing is also an issue for the survivors of labor trafficking as well as their dependent family. As proposed by Owens et al. (2014), "[g]iven that survivors lack credit history and are often unable to work legally for months, service provider organizations could pay the cost of the apartment and then use a sliding scale of payment until survivors are back on their feet" (p. XVII). Social service providers in St. Louis and the bi-state area are currently working towards creating a system of housing for survivors of sex trafficking. A similar model or a model similar to that proposed by Owens et al. could be established for survivors of labor trafficking. Access to grant funding streams earmarked for labor trafficked people is imperative in order for this to occur.

Beyond the immediate needs of housing and communication, social service providers need to "increase [the] availability of trauma-informed, linguistically and culturally competent mental health care" (ibid.). As was previously stated with regards to sex trafficking, victim centered care is central for survivors of labor trafficking. Many of the victims of labor trafficking have been traumatized by constant threats by the trafficker. These threats include, but are not limited to, physical threats to the individual, physical threats to the family, economic threats, and deportation. These threats can overlap one another, making the perfect storm of fear.

As Owen et al. noted (2014), "[m]any victims of labor trafficking have come to the United States in search of opportunity because such opportunity does not exist in their home countries. It is common for these individuals to have acquired significant debt along the way, some even using their property or homes as leverage, and they cannot afford to return home until these debts are repaid" (p. 195). Traffickers are fully aware of these fears, and use these fears as leverage to keep the victims from reporting their victimization. Therefore, those that have been identified need to be assured a sense of protection, and must be provided with the proper services to assist in the healing process. The fears used to maintain bondage are not going to dissipate upon identification, and therefore, social service providers must be equipped to deal with the psychological issues unique to survivors of labor trafficking.

Implications for Law Enforcement

Sex Trafficking

The research was promising in the area of sex trafficking, showing progress with law enforcement efforts; being made, specifically, in victim identification, the shifting of attitudes, and training. Almost every officer we talked with was concerned with sex trafficking and what measures needed to be taken to alleviate the problem. Although, some believed that sex trafficking was not as prevalent as the media portrayed, the majority felt that it was happening in St. Louis and the bi-state area, usually in conjunction with other underlying criminal offenses. However, there are still issues that need to be addressed to better improve the identification and protection of victims of sex trafficking.

The first measure that law enforcement needs to consider is the age of the identified victim. Many of those officers interviewed focused their attention on child victims or juvenile prostitution. However, adult prostitutes were generally treated as criminals under an assumption that they voluntarily entered the world of prostitution after the age of consent. One officer interviewed was more aware of the need to focus investigations of adult prostitutes not only on their current criminality, but their history and how long they had been in "the life":

> Until probably five years ago, my attitude was the same ... Okay, well, there's this prostitute, arrest her, put her in jail, and move on about your day ... I never stopped to think about that ... there's a whole lot more dynamics to it ... [T]he girls that we deal with ... most of them were molested as children ... started prostituting around fourteen, fifteen years old, and then you're coming in contact with them sometimes ... at that twenty-five [to] thirty-year-old range, and they've already been through a lot ... They get mentally beat down, physically beat down, families are threatened, children are threatened, all those kinds of things ...

Given this officer's awareness, he began working with his department as well as other departments in the community to start recognizing these patterns of abuse and the relationship to adult prostitution. It is imperative that all officers look at the history of the adult prostitute that may have just been arrested, and view her/him as a potential victim of human trafficking who has been and is still being exploited by her/his trafficker.

In addition to not creating a dichotomy of "criminal" and "victim" based upon age, it is important to be respectful of the potential human trafficking victim. One officer has recently learned at a training of how important that relationship of respect is when attempting to assist a potential victim: "One of the survivors ... started prostituting at fourteen ... But this policeman just kept treating her nice ... and then finally one day, she just ... fifteen years later when she was ... thirty years old, she finally decided ... I'm gonna listen to what [that police officer] said and ... it worked." Fifteen years this woman was working as a prostitute, going through a cycle of arrests. Yet the officers she had contact with maintained an open door of assistance, and although it took her fifteen years, she did not get lost in the criminal justice system once she turned eighteen. There needs to be an avenue of trust between law enforcement and victims. If they have only been harassed by police, by getting arrested repeatedly, once they are ready to reveal their victimization, they might not feel they have a legal outlet. Attitudes need to change from punishing "the criminal" to helping victims get out of the life to become survivors. Although some departments we talked with were working on changing offi- cers' perceptions, it remains a difficult barrier to break when there is such a fine line between "criminal" and "victim," at least as cur- rently defined by prostitution policy.

Aside from changing attitudes and the focus on age, the re- search showed that although the officers were receiving training in identifying victims of sex trafficking, there was a range of percep- tions about the trainings, who should conduct the trainings, and who should receive the trainings. The perceptions of the trainings ranged from being extremely useful to just a stack of PowerPoint slides to put in a desk. Those that found the trainings useful al- ready had some interest in identifying victims of sex trafficking, and so it became a bit of "preaching to the choir" mentality. On the other hand, those that found the trainings useless also believed that the few cases of sex trafficking prosecuted were fringe cases and that the idea of human trafficking was just a new hot topic. Additionally, officers felt that it would be more beneficial for peo- ple from their own field to conduct the trainings so that they could get first-hand information as to what they may encounter. Others enjoyed the collaboration between social service providers and law enforcement. Lastly, some officers felt that only those that would be participating in undercover investigations should be receiving the trainings while others believed that every person in the acad- emy should be receiving the training. Given these various attitudes and perceptions of training, the research shows that attitudes of law enforcement should be addressed through continued training, to show how shifting attitudes and education about sex trafficking will only benefit investigations. How the trainings can be altered to shift the officers' attitudes towards a recognition of importance and how they can better look beneath the surface will be discussed later in the chapter. However, before discussing trainings, it is im- portant to look at the implications of our research for law enforce- ment with regards to labor trafficking.

Labor Trafficking

Those individuals in the legal arena interviewed for this project fell into one of two camps with regards to their awareness of labor trafficking; either they did not believe labor trafficking occurred in St. Louis and the bi-state area, or they were aware of the existence of labor trafficking but did not have any investigative measures in place to identify and protect victims. That being said, there are a number of measures that need to be taken by law enforcement officials to ensure the safety and security of survivors of labor trafficking. First and foremost, they need to come to terms with the fact that St. Louis and the bi-state area have all of the necessary components required for labor trafficking to transpire. For example, in Missouri alone, 50% of agriculture and the livestock industry require some form of cheap or migrant labor. There exists insulated immigrant communities on which traffickers can prey. Lastly, one of the most overlooked issues regarding labor trafficking is that there is a cross-connection between labor trafficking and sex trafficking. In one sense, sex trafficking victims may also be labor trafficking victims. In another sense, where labor trafficking is evident, there is generally sex trafficking occurring in the same area. This symbiotic relationship occurs partly due to similar demands; the demand for underground cheap (or unpaid) labor coincides with a demand for prostitution (Heil, 2012). Thus, as law enforcement officials are investigating sex trafficking cases, they should be aware of the possibility of related or overlapping labor trafficking cases.

Beyond the general knowledge of the prevalence of labor trafficking, it is imperative that actors in the legal arena be more cooperative with the foreign nationals with whom they may come into contact. In isolated communities where labor trafficking is extremely prevalent, research has shown that a visible, open police force was more conducive with identification and cooperation from labor trafficking survivors (see Heil, 2012). Therefore, rather than seeing the criminality associated with illegal immigration, law officers need to look beyond the surface and investigate the indicators associated with labor trafficking, which include physical abuse, someone else holding documents, or someone else doing all of the speaking. Although these indicators may not necessarily lead to a labor trafficking case, it is better for the first responder to err on the side of caution. If the victim is immediately criminalized, the fears of deportation that the trafficker has been leveling become very real, and victims are not going to approach law enforcement with regards to their victimization.

Part of the visibility and open law enforcement strategy includes proactive policing. Rather than waiting for a call or in the process of everyday investigations, officers need to be visible in the immigrant communities. Only one local level police officer interviewed for the project mentioned the movement towards working with the immigrant communities in a proactive manner. According to this officer, " ... we just did an awareness thing and ... talked with ... [the] Hispanic leadership group.... What we're seeing ... is you've got a very diverse groups (sic) of people so naturally they don't trust the police depending on what country they're from ... Then you've got ... immigration status issues which keeps people from coming forward ..." This officer was aware of the problems associated with labor trafficking and immigration, and was working towards building the bridge between law enforcement and the immigrant communities. However, this was only one department of those that were interviewed in the bi-state area that were openly working on proactive policing and becoming visible in these insular communities.

Aside from visibility, there are other strategies in which the police could use to build relationships with the immigrant population. Some of these include participating language classes so that there is not a translation issue. As stated, one of the indicators of labor trafficking is having another person speak or translate for the victim when questioned. Many times, the translator is the trafficker and giving false information. If law officials were fluent in an additional language, this could clarify any false reporting and better assist in identifying a trafficking situation. Beyond translating, proactive strategies that have proved beneficial in other communities throughout the United States include talking with the migrant laborers when they enter a town and provide them with information regarding human trafficking (see Heil, 2012). This information sharing could also be conducted in the immigrant communities throughout the year. Not only will this assist in identifying victims, but it will also create an avenue of communication and openness. Survivors of labor trafficking may be more willing to report their victimization to an officer they have had a previous, albeit positive, encounter.

It is important for local level law enforcement officials to work with federal agencies better fit to assist in investigating labor trafficking cases. Although local level officers work closely with the U.S. Immigration and Customs Enforcement (ICE), and the Federal Bureau of Investigations (FBI) if a case of labor trafficking is identified, Owens et al. (2014) suggest that "[e]fforts should ... be made to better coordinate with the Department of Labor to file back wage claims for trafficking survivors" (p. XVII). We agree that the collection of wages and damages is important in the recovery process, but we also believe that building a relationship with the Department of Labor, as well as the Department of State, would assist in separating cases of wage-per-hour violations, visa violations, and labor trafficking cases.

Lastly, actors in the legal arena need to be aware of the nontraditional forms of labor trafficking. As of now, in St. Louis and the bi-state area, those officers that are aware of labor trafficking are investigating orchards, restaurants, livestock factories, construction sites, and lawn care companies. They are also following up on tips in which there is the possibility of hiring undocumented workers. Unfortunately, not all labor trafficking involved foreign nationals, and traffickers are widening their scope of exploitation. For example, traveling sales crews (e.g., selling magazines, candy, cleaning supplies, etc.) have recruited individuals with an employment pitch, only to transport these individuals away from friends and family, isolating them from anyone in the community, and forcing them to work regardless of weather or health conditions (Polaris Project, 2007). According to the Polaris Project, the traveling crews "[n]ot only is each youth responsible for a daily quota of sales, some crews are also known to create collective quotas for all the youth in each van ... First-hand reports ... indicate direct physical beatings from other van members based on being responsible for falling short of a van quota" (ibid.). Additional punishment for not making the quota is a financial penalty that creates a cycle of debt for the child or young adult. Law enforcement officials often come into contact with these youth or young adults, ticketing for "soliciting without a permit." That contact is an opportunity for law enforcement officials to ask follow-up questions to determine whether or not this child or young adult requires assistance to escape the traveling sales crew. The same holds true when law enforcement officials have contact with homeless youth or other vulnerable populations. Rather than criminalizing their activities, proactively ask questions that could indicate whether or not the individual is indebted to someone, abused, and/or exploited.

Education and Training

Education and training was highlighted by the respondents as one of the more successful endeavors of anti-trafficking efforts in the St. Louis bi-state area. While identified as successful, community awareness and training of professionals needs to be ongoing. Consequently, one important implication of the research findings is increased funding for expanded and ongoing education and training of the general community, social service providers, law enforcement, and front line workers. First, in order to address high turnover in social services and in policing, continuous training is necessary. Second, identification through citizen awareness, as well as training of professionals trafficked people are more likely to come into contact with, is only possible if such individuals are trained to recognize potential signs. Hotel workers, healthcare workers, cable, gas, electric and phone workers, cab drivers, truckers, and K–12 teachers and staff are among those in need of continued training. Social service providers in the areas of domestic violence, children's services, rape and sexual assault, and crisis line workers also need ongoing training. Law enforcement also needs continued training, and in particular, interactive training with use of scenarios may be important, as this is what law enforcement described to us as what officers wanted and would find helpful. Third, community awareness is important in garnering the public and consequent political support that is needed to increase funding streams for badly needed services to labor trafficked and sex trafficked people. Continued community education at schools, colleges and universities, faith based organizations, and other community organizations is important. Community awareness doesn't just increase the likelihood of citizen-tips, it also creates a community of support. When people care about human trafficking, politicians start to care because they want their vote. The authors recommend community activism and political support surrounding access to funding streams for the multiple recommendations depicted in this chapter.

Based upon the issues uncovered related to bias directed toward LGBTQ people, the authors recommend that cultural competency and awareness of issues specifically impacting LGBTQ people who are trafficked should be incorporated directly into the main anti-trafficking training curriculum, particularly for police and social service providers. Further, Safe Zone training, or something similar, should be mandatory for all social service providers. Safe Zone training works to familiarize trainees with basic use of LGBTQ friendly language, such as avoiding heterosexist language, as well as other related elements of cultural competency. In addition, inclusive language should be used on all media of social service organizations—such as websites, brochures, training materials, etc.

As the research findings also found truancy to be a risk factor, we recommend training in schools for teachers and staff to note truant youth and begin the process of contacting parents and related social services. In St. Louis City, the Juvenile Division of the Family Courts worked with city schools in addressing truancy lists; other sites with similar contextual dynamics may also benefit from this format. Further, direct outreach from social service providers, collaborating with schools and truancy officers, may also prove an effective model, although more research is needed in this area. Such groups could use truancy lists as tools for outreach to these at-risk kids. Social service providers, truancy officers, and the juvenile division may benefit from developing formal collaboration. Importantly, we also recommend prevention through education and outreach in at-risk schools. Education about sex trafficking for youth beginning in middle school in high-risk school districts with high truancy, student population turnover, teacher turnover, and dropout rates is also recommended, as individuals are typically trafficked in their early teens. Prevention prior to the age of sex trafficking may be important in guiding prevention. Importantly, as African Americans are overrepresented as sex trafficking victims, increased outreach, education, and training in predominately African American communities in at-risk school districts may be an important aspect of prevention. While anyone can be a victim, and survivors in the St. Louis area come from all demographic groups and regions, the disproportionately higher victimization rates of African American women and girls overall cannot be ignored. Colorblindness in this area amounts to covert racism and the perpetuation of the victimization of Black women and girls.

Lastly, labor trafficking needs to be highlighted in the trainings as an issue of concern in St. Louis and the bi-state area. The limited material that is being taught covers the charges and penalties associated with visa violations. This discussion needs to go beyond visa violations and provide information regarding the indicators of labor trafficking as well as the vulnerable populations. Among all of those interviewed for this project, we found that only in Southern Missouri were police receiving training that encompassed more than visa violations, and emphasized the need to identify victims of labor trafficking, specifically in the agricultural sector. Trainings that involve a comprehensive discussion of labor trafficking in its various forms needs to go beyond agricultural communities, and be included in human trafficking education in all jurisdictions, both within our study population and the United States in general. Moreover, farmers need training, in order to identify trafficking that may be facilitated by crew leaders on their own farms and orchards. Expanded outreach in rural agricultural areas in hotels where migrants may be staying, healthcare clinics, and other community organizations is also needed, in addition to continued and expanded education and awareness of labor trafficking in the urban and suburban areas of the bi-state area.

Implications for Policy

The shift towards introducing policy that protects victims of human trafficking has gained momentum in the past decade. In the summer of 2014, the House of Representatives passed eight bills that create new laws and update existing ones to help law enforcement and communities combat human trafficking. These bills include:

H.R. 2283, the Human Trafficking Prioritization Act— elevates the "Office to Monitor and Combat Trafficking" to bureau status so the office reports directly to the Secretary of State.

H.R. 4449, the Human Trafficking Prevention Act—requires federal employees around the globe get trained in combating human trafficking.

H.R. 4980, the Preventing Sex Trafficking and Strengthening Families Act—requires states to modify foster care standards and goals to increase permanent living arrangements among foster children and requires states to implement programs to prevent sex trafficking among at risk foster children.

H.R. 5076, the Enhancing Services for Runaway and Homeless Victims of Youth Trafficking Act of 2014—extends grants to nonprofit private agencies who provide street-based services to runaways and the homeless at risk of being trafficked. Additionally, requires HHS give priority to training and researching the effects of trafficking, and strategies for working with runaways and homeless youth victims.

H.R. 5081, the Strengthening Child Welfare Response to Trafficking Act of 2014—expands the requirements for states that receive grants for child protective services to include trafficking victims, identifying and assessing reports of trafficked victims, training workers to identify victims, and identifying services for referral to address the needs of victims.

H.R. 5111—improves the response to victims of child sex trafficking by updating the Missing Children's Assistance

Act to replace the term "child prostitution" with "child sex
trafficking, including child prostitution" in the reporting
categories in the National Center for Missing and Exploited Children (NCMEC) CyberTipline so the public
knows to report any case involving child prostitution or
child sex trafficking to the tip line.
H.R. 5116—directs the Secretary of Homeland Security to
train Department of Homeland Security personnel on how
to effectively deter, detect, disrupt, and prevent human
trafficking, and requires training programs for TSA, Customs and Border Protection, and other departments so employees can deter, detect, and disrupt human trafficking.
**H.R. 5135, the Human Trafficking Prevention, Interven-
tion, and Recovery Act of 2014**—requires all federal and
state law enforcement to report on efforts to combat trafficking domestically. Additionally, this bill allows Justice
Department grants to be used to support organizations
that provide housing to trafficking victims. (Davis, 2014).

Obviously, the passage of such bills greatly increases the protection
of many identified victims, as well as protects vulnerable youth
from being enticed by traffickers. However, the majority of these
bills focus on sex trafficking, and more specifically, child sex trafficking. The bills need to extend the definition of human trafficking to include victims of labor trafficking and adult victims. Although some of the above stated bills use the inclusive term
"human trafficking," members of Congress have openly stated to
the first author that they were not considering labor trafficking
with the passage of these bills. That lens needs to change and needs
to policy makers need to assure the protection of all victims of
human trafficking regardless of age or type of victimization.

Aside from creating more inclusive policies, the human trafficking laws that prosecutors must abide by need to be re-examined so
that the "coercion" component is not so difficult to prove. Missouri
has already re-worded their state's human trafficking law so that
coercion is more easily identified. For example, blackmail and
threat of blackmail are included in the definition of coercion in the

Missouri statute. Federally, the human trafficking law needs to adopt similar language so that federal prosecutors are not compelled to charge a trafficker with a lesser offense merely because the coercion element is not beyond a reasonable doubt. Rewording the law will not only allow for more federal prosecutions of human trafficking, but it will also help us get a more accurate representation of human trafficking in the United States based on the number of prosecutions.

Because most of the policies specifically address sex trafficking, a discussion of general prostitution policy is necessary. Both abolitionists and neoliberals agree that criminalization of prostitutes is harmful, albeit for differing reasons. Abolitionists are those who wish to eradicate all prostitution, as it is viewed as harmful to human beings, particularly women and girls (Ekberg, 2004; Madden-Dempsey, 2011; Kotrla, 2010). All prostitutes are viewed as victims, who either make a socially conditioned "choice" to engage in prostitution, or who are coerced into prostitution. Prostitution and sex trafficking are inseparable in their victimizing nature, and are consequently viewed as one and the same in abolitionist perspective. Abolitionist models, also referred to as the "Swedish" model, criminalize clients and traffickers, who are viewed as victimizers, but prostitutes are not criminalized, as they are viewed as victims (Ekberg, 2004; Madden-Dempsey, 2011; Outshoorn, 2010; Nichols, 2015). Neoliberals oppose criminalization of prostitution as well, but under the ideology that prostitution is a legitimate form of work. Neoliberals hold that prostitution and sex trafficking are distinct—prostitution can take the form of sex work or sex trafficking. Neoliberals support rights to sex work, while opposing sex trafficking. Prostitutes are only seen as victims if they are unwilling participants in commercial sexual exchanges (Weitzer, 2010; Madden-Dempsey, 2011; Nichols, 2015). Further, neoliberals point out that decriminalization of prostitution offers sex workers access to legal recourse for their victimization without fear of being arrested, fined, or otherwise re-victimized by the justice system. Both groups agree that prostitutes should not be criminalized, and sex traffickers should be criminalized, but they differ on the issue of clients. Abolitionists believe buyers should be criminalized to the full extent of the law, in order to curtail demand, which is viewed as the root cause of sex trafficking. In contrast, neoliberals believe that clients should be allowed the right to purchase sex acts from adults who are willing sex workers. These groups continue to engage in highly ideologically charged heated debates, both in the academic and public discourse.

Based upon the research findings, the authors recommend addressing this overlapping area of agreement, by not criminalizing prostitutes. Criminalization serves to further victimize those who prostitute or who are prostituted. First, a felony prostitution charge can result in a lifetime of stigmatization and marginalization from legitimate employment, resulting in blocked access to basic needs and control of one's own future. This is corroborated by other research (see Lloyd, 2012; Oselin, 2014). Inaccessible shelter or housing, denial of welfare, and blocked access to food stamps function in tandem to provide a bleak future for sex trafficking survivors as well, who are often criminalized and denied these things because of the felony record. Further, prostitution-related fines reproduce sex trafficking situations. In order to pay the fines, individuals return to prostitution, with the coercive element in this case, ironically, coming from the criminal justice system. Further, when prostituted people are criminalized, they lack legal recourse for their victimization, and trust between prostitutes and police is undermined (Nichols, 2010, 2015). This prevents identification of sex trafficking victimization, and barriers to accessing services that may facilitate recovery.

Conclusion

Human trafficking is not an activity that only occurs in economically devastated countries, or in large cities, or in border towns. Human trafficking occurs in virtually every corner of the United States. Traffickers prey on vulnerable migrants looking for work. They manipulate children looking to fill a void in their life, whether it be love, money, or just attention. They exploit adults who are economically disadvantaged who have few opportunities or choices. Traffickers are not deterred by the punishments associated with trafficking charges, if they are even charged with a trafficking offense, as this is a multi-billion-dollar industry (Heil & Nichols, 2014). They are able to continuously make a profit as they repeatedly sell their "product," skillfully making a commodity of human beings. Human trafficking cannot be eradicated; the best that can be done is to make it more difficult for traffickers to recruit and sell new victims, and to address the needs of survivors. This can be done through continuous education and training of law enforcement officials, prosecutors, social service providers, and members of the community, as well as shifts in policy and practices.

Unfortunately, as traffickers encounter legal and social barriers, they will change their tactics, as well as how they can exploit their victims (Heil, 2012; Heil & Nichols, 2014; Busch-Armendariz, 2009; Farrell et al., 2012). Therefore, those involved in anti-trafficking efforts need to think outside of the box and consider how else the traffickers could make money beyond the already identified techniques. The traffickers are already thinking of ways to increase their profit, so it is imperative that social service providers and law enforcement officials get into the mindset of the trafficker. Human trafficking will continue to evolve, and we as a society need to start discussion some of the lesser known trafficking offenses, such as the selling of organs, adoption, and begging and panhandling. We need to widen our net of understanding as to how a trafficker can profit off of their victims so that we do not lose footing on the progress that we have made. Once again, education, training, and communication between law enforcement, social service providers, and the community is central to combatting human trafficking.

References

Bennett, L. and L. Goodman (2005). Risk factors for reabuse in intimate partner violence: A cross-disciplinary critical review. *Trauma Violence & Abuse*, 6: 141–175.

Bennett-Catteneo, L. and L. Goodman (2010). Through the lens of therapeutic jurisprudence: The relationship between empowerment in the court system and well-being for intimate partner violence victims. *Journal of Interpersonal Violence*, 25, 481–502.

Busch-Armendariz, N., M. Nsonwu, and L. Cook Heffron (2009). "Understanding Human Trafficking: Development of Typologies of Traffickers PHASE II." *First Annual Interdisciplinary Conference on Human Trafficking, 2009*, October. http:// digitalcommons.unl.edu/humtraffconf/9.

Clawson, H., N. Dutch, and M. Cummings (2006). Law Enforcement Response to Human Trafficking and the Implications for Victims: Current Practices and Lessons Learned. U.S. Department of Justice.

Clawson, H. J., N. Dutch, S. Lopez, and S. Tiapula (2008). Prosecuting Human Trafficking Cases: Lessons Learned and Promising Practices. U.S. Department of Justice.

Crouch, E. (2013, May 24). Only a few students defy St. Louis school's high turnover rate. Retrieved from www.stltoday.com.

Crouch, E. (2013, September 11). Challenges in St. Louis schools have some teachers quitting. Retrieved from www.stltoday.com.

Curtis, R. (2008). The Commercial Sexual Exploitation of Children in New York City Volume One: The CSEC Population in

New York City Size, Characteristics, and Needs. Center for Court Innovation.

Davis, R. (2014). Rep. Davis: House Continues Work to Prevent Human Trafficking. Retrieved from rodneydavis.house.gov.

Dempsey, M.M. (2010). *Sex Trafficking and Criminalization: In Defense of Feminist Abolitionism.* SSRN Scholarly Paper ID 1710264. Rochester, NY: Social Science Research Network. http://papers.ssrn.com/abstract=1710264.

Doezema, J. (1999). "Loose Women or Lost Women? The Re-Emergence of the Myth of White Slavery in Contemporary Discourses of Trafficking in Women." *Gender Issues* 18 (1): 23–50. doi:10.1007/s12147-999-0021-9.

———. (2005). "Now You See Her, Now You Don't: Sex Workers at the UN Trafficking Protocol Negotiation." *Social & Legal Studies* 14 (1): 61–89. doi:10.1177/0964663905049526.

Downs, R. (2013). "Hungry and Broke but Have a Drug Felony? MO Still One of Few States That Says: Starve" Retrieved from http://blogs.riverfronttimes.com.

Draper, B. (2009, August 16). Mo. RICO charges for 1st human trafficking case. The Seattle Times. Retrieved from http://seattletimes.com.

Eden House. 2014. The Nashville Model. Retrieved from http://edenhousenola.org/.

Edmond, T., L. Sloan and D. McCarty (2004). Sexual abuse survivors' perceptions of the effectiveness of EMDR and eclectic therapy. *Research on Social Work Practice,* 14(4), 249–258.

Ekberg, G. (2004). "The Swedish Law That Prohibits the Purchase of Sexual Services Best Practices for Prevention of Prostitution and Trafficking in Human Beings." *Violence against Women* 10 (10): 1187–1218. doi: 10.1177/1077801204268647.

End Slavery Cincinnati (2014) Red flags and indicators. Retrieved from http://www.endslaverycincinnati.org.

Farrell, A. (2013). "Environmental and Institutional Influences on Police Agency Responses to Human Trafficking." *Police Quarterly*, July, 1098611113495050. doi:10.1177/1098611113495050.

Farrell, A., J. McDevitt, R. Pfeffer, S. Fahy, C. Owens, M. Dank, and W. Adams (2012). *Identifying challenges to improve the investigation and prosecution of state and local human trafficking cases.* Washington, DC: National Institute of Justice.

Fazal, F. (May 2013). Michael Johnson, Samantha Ginocchio charged for selling girls for sex. Retrieved from www.ksdk.com.

Foa, E., E. Hembree, S. Cahill, S. Rauch, D. Riggs, and N. Feeny (2005). Randomized trial of prolonged exposure for posttraumatic stress disorder with and without cognitive structuring: Outcome at academic and community clinics. *Journal of consulting and Clinical Psychology*, 73(5): 953–964.

Foa, E., C. McLean, S. Capaldi, and D. Rosenfield (2013). Prolonged exposure vs supportive counseling for sexual abuse-related PTSD in adolescent girls: A randomized clinical trial. *JAMA* 310, (24): 2650–2657.

Fritch, A. and S. Lynch (2008). Group treatment for adult survivors of interpersonal trauma. *Journal of Psychological Trauma*, 7 (3): 145–169.

Galovski, T., L.M. Blain, J.M. Mott, L. Elwood, and T. Houle (2012). Manualized therapy for PTSD: Flexing the structure of cognitive processing therapy. *Journal of Consulting and Clinical Psychology* Vol. 80, (6): 968–981.

GEMS. Girls Education and Mentoring Services (2014). Retrieved from http://www.gems-girls.org/.

Heil, E.C. (2012). *Sex slaves and serfs: The dynamics of human trafficking in a small Florida town.* Boulder, CO: First Forum Press.

Heil, E.C. and A.J. Nichols (2014). A Theoretical Discussion of the Potential Problems Associated with Targeted Policing and the Eradication of Sex Trafficking in the United States. *Contemporary Justice Review.* 17 (4) doi: 10.1080/10282580.2014 .980966.

Hepburn, S. and R.J. Simon (2010). "Hidden in Plain Sight: Human Trafficking in the United States." *Gender Issues* 27 (1–2): 1–26. doi:10.1007/s12147-010-9087-7.

Hopper, E. (2004). "Underidentification of Human Trafficking Victims in the United States." *Journal of Social Work Research and Evaluation* 5 (2): 125–36.

Hoyle, C., M. Bosworth, and M. Dempsey (2011). "Labeling the Victims of Sex Trafficking: Exploring the Borderland between Rhetoric and Reality." *Social & Legal Studies* 20 (3): 313–29. doi:10.1177/0964663911405394.

H.R. 4225, SAVE Act (2014).

Hughes, D. M. (2005). "Race and Prostitution." Unpublished manuscript. University of Rhode Island, http://www.uri.edu/artsci/wms/hughes.

Illinois General Assembly (2012). Trafficking in Persons, Involuntary Servitude, and Related Offenses. 720 ILCS5/10-9.

International Institute of St. Louis (2013). http://www.iistl.org/aboutus.html.

Jordan, J. (2010). *Relational Cultural Therapy*. American Psychological Association. Washington D.C.

Kotrla, K. (2010). Domestic minor sex trafficking in the United States. *Social Work*, 55: 181–187.

Kulkarni, S., H. Bell, and D. Rhodes (2012). Back to basics. *Violence against Women*, 18: 85.

Legal Service of Eastern Missouri (2014). http://www.lsem.org.

Lloyd, R. (2012). *Girls like us: Fighting for a world where girls are not for sale*. Harper Perennial, New York, NY.

MacKinnon, C. A. (2004). Pornography as trafficking. *Michigan Journal of International Law*. 26, 993.

Marcus, A., A. Horning, R. Curtis, J. Sanson, and E. Thompson (2014). "Conflict and Agency among Sex Workers and Pimps A Closer Look at Domestic Minor Sex Trafficking." *The AN-

NALS of the American Academy of Political and Social Science 653 (1): 225–46. doi: 10.1177/0002716214521993.

Martin, L., A. Pierce, S. Peyton, A.I. Gabilondo, and G. Tulpule (2014). "Mapping the Market for Sex with Trafficked Minor Girls in Minneapolis: Structures, Functions, and Patterns." Full report: Preliminary Findings (available at uroc.umn .edu/sextrafficking).

Mendelsohn, M., J. Herman, E. Schatzow, M. Coco, D. Kallivayalil, and J. Levitan (2011). *The trauma recovery group: A guide for practitioners.* The Guilford Press, New York, NY.

Missouri Department of Elementary and Secondary Education. (2013). http://dese.mo.gov/school-data.

Missouri General Assembly (2013). Sexual Trafficking of a Child. Chapter 566.212.

Missouri General Assembly (2013). Trafficking for the Purposes of Sexual Exploitation. Chapter 566.209.

Moossy, R. (2009). *Sex trafficking: Identifying cases and victims* (National Institute of Justice Journal No. 262). National Institute of Justice, Washington, D.C.

National Child Traumatic Stress Network (2006). Retrieved from www.nctsnet.org/.

National Human Trafficking Resource Center (2014). Retrieved from http://www.polarisproject.org.

National Resource Center for Permanency and Family Connections (2012). "Toolkit for Practitioners/Researchers Working with Lesbian, Gay, Bisexual, Transgender, and Queer/Questioning (LGBTQ) Runaway and Homeless Youth (RHY)." Retrieved from www.nrcpfc.org/is/LGBTQ-Children-and-Youth-in-ChildWelfare.html.

Nichols, A. J. (2013). Meaning-Making and Domestic Violence Victim Advocacy: An Examination of Feminist Identities, Ideologies, and Practices. *Feminist Criminology* 8(3):177–201.

Nichols, A. J. (2014). *Feminist Advocacy: Gendered Organizations in Community-Based Responses to Domestic Violence.* Lexington Books, Lanham, MD.

Nichols, A. J. (Forthcoming 2015). *Sex Trafficking in the United States: Theory, Research, and Policy.* Columbia University Press, New York, NY.

Nichols, A. J. and E. C. Heil (2014). "Challenges to Identifying and Prosecuting Sex Trafficking Cases in the Midwest United States." *Feminist Criminology,* doi:10.1177/1557085113519490.

Oselin, S. (2014). *Leaving Prostitution: Getting Out and Staying Out of Sex Work.* NYT Press, New York, NY.

Outshoorn, J. (2005). "The Political Debates on Prostitution and Trafficking of Women." *Social Politics: International Studies in Gender, State and Society* 12 (1): 141–55. http://muse.jhu.edu/journals/social_politics/v012/12.1outshoorn.html.

Owens, C., M. Dank, J. Breaux, I. Bañuelos, A. Farrell, R. Pfeffer, K. Bright, R. Heitsmith, J. McDevitt (2014). Understanding the Organization, Operation, and Victimization Process of Labor Trafficking in the United States. Retrieved from www.urban.org.

Polaris Project (2007). Traveling Sales Crews: What we know so Far. Retrieved from http://www.travelingsalescrews.info/pdf/Traveling%20Sales%20Crews%20AAG.pdf.

Polaris Project (2013). 2013 Analysis of State Human Trafficking Laws. Retrieved from www.polarisproject.org.

Proud, K. (2013, June 13). St. Louis named the "most sinful city in America." Retrieved from http://news.stlpublicradio.org.

Raasch, C. (2014, May 3). In Offensive against Sex Trafficking, Ann Wagner Steps into Controversial Realm. St. Louis Post Dispatch. Retrieved from www.stltoday.com.

Raphael, J. (2008). "Pimp Control and Violence: Domestic Sex Trafficking of Chicago Women and Girls. DePaul College of Law. Retrieved from www.law.depaul.edu/family.

Raphael, J. and B. Myers-Powell (2008). From Victims to Victim-izers: Interviews with 25 Ex-Pimps in Chicago. DePaul College of Law. Raphael 2010family_law_center_report-final.pdf.

Raphael, J., J. Reichert, J. and M. Powers (2010). Pimp control and violence: Domestic sex trafficking of Chicago women and girls. *Women & Criminal Justice*, 20: 89–104.

Reid, J. A. (2010). "Doors Wide Shut: Barriers to the Successful Delivery of Victim Services for Domestically Trafficked Minors in a Southern U.S. Metropolitan Area." *Women & Criminal Justice* 20 (1–2): 147–66. doi:10.1080/08974451003641206.

Rescue and Restore Coalition. 2014. https://www.acf.hhs.gov/programs/orr/resource/about-rescue-restore.

Rizvi, S., D. Vogt, and P. Resick (2009). Cognitive and affective predictors of treatment outcomes in cognitive processing therapy and prolonged exposure for posttraumatic stress disorder. *Behaviour Research and Therapy*, 47 (9): 737–743.

Schaeffer-Grabiel, F. (2010). "Sex Trafficking as the 'New Slave Trade'?" *Sexualities* 13 (2): 153–60. doi:10.1177/1363460709359234.

Schubert, S. and C. Lee (2009). Adult PTSD and its treatment with EMDR: A review of controversies, evidence, and theoretical knowledge. *Journal of EMDR Practice and Research*, 3 (3): 117–132.

Smith, L., S.H. Vardaman, and M. Snow, M (2009). *The national report on DMST*. Shared Hope International, Vancouver, WA.

State of Missouri (2011). House Bill No. 214.

Stop Advertising Victims of Exploitation Act. Retrieved from http://wagner.house.gov/notforsale.

Trafficking of Victims Protection Act (2000). PUBLIC LAW 106–386—OCT. 28, 2000.

Ulibarri, M. D., S. A. Strathdee, R. Lozada, C. Magis-Rodriguez, H. Amaro, P. O'Campo, and T. L. Patterson (2014). "Prevalence and Correlates of Client-Perpetrated Abuse among Female Sex Workers in Two Mexico–U.S. Border Cities." *Violence against Women* 20 (4): 427–45. doi:10.1177/10778012145 28582.

United States of America v. Abrorkhodja Askarkhodjaev (2011). Case No. 09-00143-01-CR-W-ODS.

United States of America v. David Keith (2013). Case Nos. 07-6265, 07-6266.

U.S. Attorney's Office, Eastern District of Missouri. 2014. http://www.justice.gov/usao/moe/.

U.S. Attorney's Office, Southern District of Illinois. 2014. www.justice.gov/usao/ils/.

U.S. Census Bureau. 2014. http://quickfacts.census.gov/qfd/states/29/29510.html.

U.S. Department of Justice (2000). 18. U.S. Code § 1581–1594.

U.S. Department of Justice (2006). *Report on activities to combat human trafficking fiscal years 2001–2005.* Retrieved from http://www.ansarilawfirm.com/docs/DOJ-Report-on-Activities-to-Combat-Human-Trafficking.pdf.

U.S. Department of Justice (2012a). Local Landscaping Company And Owner Sentenced Involving The Employment Of Illegal Aliens. Retrieved from www.justice.gov.

U.S. Department of Justice (2012b). Local Industrial Supply Company Sentenced For Employing Illegal Aliens. Retrieved from www.justice.gov.

U.S. Department of Justice (2013). Duren Banks and Tracey Kyckelhahn, *Characteristics of Suspected Human Trafficking Incidents,* 2008–2010, 1, Washington, DC, Retrieved from http://www.bjs.gov/content/pub/pdf/cshti0810.pdf.

Weitzer, R. (2010). *The Movement to Criminalize Sex Work in the United States.* SSRN Scholarly Paper ID 1558068. Social Science Research Network, Rochester, NY. Retrieved from http://papers.ssrn.com/abstract=1558068.

Williamson, C. and M. Prior (2009). "Domestic Minor Sex Trafficking: A Network of Underground Players in the Midwest." *Journal of Child & Adolescent Trauma* 2 (1): 46–61. doi:10.1080/19361520802702191.

Wilson, J. M., and E. Dalton (2008). "Human Trafficking in the Heartland Variation in Law Enforcement Awareness and Response." *Journal of Contemporary Criminal Justice* 24 (3): 296–313. doi:10.1177/1043986208318227.

Zweig, J. and M. Burt (2007). Predicting women's perceptions of domestic violence and sexual assault agency helpfulness: What matters to program clients? *Violence against Women* 13:1149–1178.

Index